Berry-Hill

Janay Wong

Everett Shinn:
The Spectacle of Life

BERRY-HILL GALLERIES, INC.

11 East 70th Street New York, New York 10021
Telephone 212.744.2300 Fax 744.2838 www.berry-hill.com

Acknowledgments

EVERETT SHINN is one of the most accomplished and celebrated artists of the Ashcan School, famous primarily for scenes of the stage and city. In recent years Shinn has been somewhat neglected by scholars and has not been for many years the subject of a fully-researched exhibition. It is accordingly with special pleasure that we present this selection, focused on his early years, which includes some well-known, familiar works on loan from New York area museums, as well some newly discovered treasures from private collections that have been lost to sight for decades. We are indebted to Janay Wong for her essay, which represents the first substantial new analysis and interpretation of Shinn in a long time; Janay is writing her doctoral dissertation on Shinn under the advisement of Dr. William H. Gerdts at the City University of New York.

We would first like to thank the lenders whose generous loans form the core of this exhibition. We are grateful to our staff who have been enormously dedicated to this project, and we would like to acknowledge particularly: Jane Yoon who thoroughly participated in all phases of this project; Minora Pacheco for her diligent coordination of the loans and Chris Ream for his beautiful installation. Janay Wong would like to express special thanks to Bruce Weber, Director of Research and Exhibitions at Berry-Hill Galleries, for his generous help, enthusiasm and guidance which have contributed significantly to this exhibition and essay. We would also like to acknowledge the individuals, listed here, who have graciously shared their time and knowledge: Jonathan Boos; Priscilla Caldwell; Ellen Cone-Busch, Curator, Planting Fields Foundation; Dr. Holly Pyne Conner, Consulting Curator of American Art, The Newark Museum; Stacey Epstein; Linda Ferber, Andrew W. Mellon Curator of American Art, Brooklyn Museum of Art; Diane Fischer, Associate Curator, The Montclair Art Museum; Rita Fraad; Abigail Booth Gerdts; Dr. William H. Gerdts, whose constant support and outstanding scholarship in the field of American art are an inspiration; Jean A. Gilmore, Registrar, The Brandywine River Museum; Robin Graham; Christopher Gray; Barbara Haskell, Curator of Prewar Art, Whitney Museum of American Art; Joseph Jacobs, Curator of Painting and Sculpture, The Newark Museum; Nancy Jarzombeck;

Kathy Keinholz, Archivist, American
Academy of Arts and Letters; Mary Ellen
Kelly; Blake Koh; Tiffany Lee; Nancy
Malloy and the staff at the Archives of
American Art; Melissa de Medeiros;
Eileen K. Morales, Manager of Collections
Access, The Museum of the City of New
York; Virginia O'Hare, Assistant Curator,
The Brandywine River Museum; Mrs.
Helen Farr Sloan; Gregory Schwartz,
Chief of Interpretation & Visitor Services,
Saint-Gaudens National Historical Site;
David Setford, Chief Curator, Norton
Museum of Art; Cameron Shay; Laura
Shirvinski; David Smith and the staff at
the New York Public Library; Theodore
Stebbins, Jr., Distinguished Fellow and
Consultative Curator of American Art,
Fogg Art Museum, Harvard University
Art Museums; Margaret Stenz; Mrs.
Vivien S. Thomas; Valerie Westcott;
Eric Widing; Dawn Michelle Wiegland,
Curator, The Charles Allis Art Museum;
Mahonri Young; W. Scott Zetrouer,
Curatorial Assistant, Gibbes Museum of
Art; and lastly the library staffs at The
Beinecke Rare Book and Manuscript
Library, Yale University, the Frick Art
Reference Library, the Helen Farr Sloan
Library at the Delaware Art Museum.

  Frederick D. Hill
  James Berry Hill
  Janay Wong

Author's Dedication

To William H. Gerdts
without whom I would not have
pursued my interest in American Art

Everett Shinn: The Spectacle of Life

By Janay Wong

FROM THE FIRST his facility and resourcefulness were evident, and in his best work these were brought to the services of a lively fancy and curiosity readily moved by the spectacle of town life, especially in its more whimsical and less known phases. The artist in him was stirred by the spectacle of the busy shopping crowds, the dismal gayety of the music halls excited his imagination, the sordid cheer of remoter dives, the bustle of the docks by day and the haggard faces of the streets at night. Of such material he made good use of the exercise of his talent…

— "Everett Shinn's Exhibition," *New York Sun,* March 11, 1903[1]

It is fitting that this exhibition, *Everett Shinn: The Spectacle of Life,* occurs at Berry-Hill Galleries in the year 2000, making it one hundred years after and 38 blocks up the avenue from Shinn's first major one-man exhibition. On view from February 26 to April 4, 1900 at the Fifth Avenue gallery, Boussod, Valadon & Co., the large debut showing was a phenomenal critical and commercial success. Of the 44 pastels exhibited, 30 were sold.[2] According to Shinn, New York socialites including Mrs. Jay Gould, Mrs. John Jacob Astor, and Mrs. Vanderbilt purchased 22 of the pictures.[3] Shinn mused, "I don't know if they liked 'em, but they'd do anything [Stanford] White — that red-headed wild man — told 'em to do."[4]

Although today Shinn is remembered primarily for his membership in the artists' group, The Eight, his contribution to American art in the early years of the 20th century was much more varied and far-reaching. Art historian Linda Ferber has noted that scholars have long acknowledged that Shinn was different from The Eight. He was the youngest of the group, the first to become famous, the one with the least attachment to the group, and the one who was perhaps the most naturally talented. Today he is best remembered for his depictions of New York streets and his spectacular representations of the theater, which distinguish him as one of the most insightful chroniclers of turn-of-the-century New York City. His work hangs in major museums and is eagerly sought by the most prominent collectors in the field.

Most artists can be said to be observers of their surroundings, but Shinn was the observer *extraordinaire*. For more than 50 years, in oil paint, pastel, red chalk, gouache, and watercolor, Shinn captured the spectacle of modern life. Shinn's keen ability to record the most salient aspects of modern city culture was recognized by the critic Henri Pène du Bois who observed, "It is necessary to say often — and it can not be said too often — that Everett Shinn's art is the most naively expressive of the activity of our time. It tells the streets, the crowds, the plays of light with an impetuous sincerity. His art of drawing is so natural, so full of ideas so human; that it gives the impression of the antique that all artists admire."[5]

Throughout much of Shinn's career he was concerned with the representation of public space as an arena where men and women from various races, classes, and social backgrounds could mingle and in so doing absorb an urban identity becoming what historian Gunter Barth has defined as "city people."[6] Shinn launched his career with low-toned pastels of urban themes and even after his trip to Europe in 1900, when his palette brightened and he was increasingly drawn to theatrical subjects, he maintained his interest in the urban spectacle as a site of public interaction. The works in this exhibition were selected for their ability to highlight the wonderment and fascination that early New Yorkers experienced as they tried to make sense of the diverse and constantly shifting turn-of-the-century environment. Shinn's subjects are remarkably different, ranging from spirited pastels of downtown street scenes such as *Park Row, Fruit Venders* (c. 1899; PLATE 9) to large oils of dancers on stage such as *Theater Scene* (c. 1906; PLATE 52). Occasionally Shinn detoured from representations of the city to work that affords a glimpse into private life, and a few of these examples are included here. At the same time that he was creating oil paintings and pastels, he also produced a large body of decorative work, which though outside the scope of this essay, is related to one example in the exhibition. In general, however,

Shinn's contribution to American art lies in his interpretation of the urban sphere as a spectacle of modern life, and it is this aspect of Shinn's career that is the focus of this exhibition.

Beginnings

Everett Shinn was born on November 6, 1876 in Pilesgrove Township, a few miles from Woodstown, New Jersey.[7] Woodstown, a residential borough situated in the northern part of Salem County, was then surrounded by rich farmland. By Shinn's own account he spent a happy childhood growing up in a fairly typical small town. He was the second of three sons born to Isaiah Conklin Shinn and Josephine Ransley Shinn, who were both Quakers. Shinn's older brother Warren was born on February 23, 1875 and his younger brother Harold was born December 2, 1883.[8] Isaiah Shinn, a great admirer of the author Edward Everett Hale, named his middle child "Everett" in honor of the writer. Shinn later become close friends with Hale's son, Edward Everett Hale, Jr. and illustrated Hale, Jr.'s book, *A Man Without a Country*.[9]

In 1887, the Shinn family moved the few miles from Pilesgrove to Woodstown into a new house on East Avenue.[10] Woodstown, and the area surrounding it, supported a large Quaker community. As a child, Shinn attended Quaker schools, first the Macaltioner Sisters' Kindergarten and later the Bacon Academy.[11] He expressed an early talent for drawing but was hesitant to display his skills in public for fear of mockery by the neighborhood children. Despite his early artistic inclination, Shinn firmly contends that he never intended to become an artist. When he left Woodstown at the age of fourteen, he enrolled not at an art school, but at the Spring Garden Institute, a technical school in Philadelphia. Founded in 1851 as a response to the demand created by the Industrial Revolution for technically trained workers, the Spring Garden Institute specialized in mechanical drawing and architecture.[12] Unbeknownst to Shinn, he was studying at the same school as John Sloan, one of the artists with whom he would later exhibit as The Eight. However, a difference in schedules prevented their meeting. After two years, Shinn left the Spring Garden Institute for a job as a draftsman at Thackery Gas Fixture Works where he spent less than a year before being fired for making drawings of hansom cabs and scurrying pedestrians in the margins of his designs of lighting fixtures. However, before dismissing him his boss advised, "Get out and do the thing you do best…. Newspaper, magazine, I would suggest…."[13] Thus, Shinn was launched on the path to his new career.

Though he lacked newspaper experience, Shinn's skill as a draftsman helped to secure him employment as an illustrator for the Philadelphia *Press*, which he joined in 1893. Shinn felt that illustration provided an invaluable education for a young artist. In his later writings and interviews he frequently expressed his regret that photography had replaced the newspaper illustrator; young artists thereby being deprived of an unparalleled learning opportunity. Recalling his experiences on the *Press* Shinn stated:

> In the Art Department of the Philadelphia Press on wobbling, ink-stained drawing boards William J. Glackens, George Luks, Everett Shinn and John Sloan went to school, a school now lamentably extinct...a school that trained memory and quick perception.[14]

The great speed demanded by the newspapers often resulted in the men leaving the office carrying nothing but envelopes, menu cards, laundry checks and other bits of paper on which to record shorthand notes of the assignment.

Although it is uncertain whether Shinn, Luks, Glackens and Sloan were ever simultaneously employed on the *Press*, the paper's fifth floor art department became their favorite place to meet.[15] As Sloan fondly remembered:

> It is not hard to recall the *Press* "art department": a dusty room with windows on Chestnut and Seventh Streets — walls plastered with caricatures of our friends and ourselves, a worn board floor, old chairs and tables close together, "no smoking" signs and a heavy odor of tabacco, and democrats (as the roaches were called in this Republican stronghold) crawling everywhere.[16]

Shinn did not stay long at the *Press* before he was hired away by the *Inquirer* for an increase in salary. At the *Inquirer* Shinn joined Sloan, who had already been on the paper's staff a year or two before Shinn's arrival. Over the next few years, newspaper hopping would become standard practice for Shinn, Luks, and Glackens, all of whom would jump between the *Press*, the *Ledger*, and the *Inquirer* each time receiving a small raise. By the time Shinn left the Philadelphia papers for the New York *World*, his salary had reached $17 a week.[17]

Newspaper illustration helped provide Shinn with a sound artistic foundation and it would continue to remain a vital resource, providing both income and ideas for future paintings. Although his style was to go through various transformations, much of his most original work reflects the urban subject matter that he first began to depict as an artist reporter. Shinn's ability to portray the prismatic effects of the city, its streets, parks, waterfront, and back alleys, as well as the diversity of its population was a skill he honed as an illustrator. His days on the newspaper also taught him to compose pictures in a manner that included all the critical details and captured the viewers' interest. Shinn's early illustrations overlap with the pastels and drawings he created independent of newspaper or magazine commissions and it is frequently difficult to separate the two categories, a situation made more complicated by the fact that Shinn often exhibited his illustrations, sometimes after reworking them.

It may have been Shinn's intention to enroll in art school while working on the *Press*, but poor timing appears have prevented him from doing so. It seems likely that his job for Thackery's was terminated either between the Pennsylvania Academy's spring and fall terms or past the deadline for spring enrollment. Fortunately, a worthwhile alternative presented itself in the form of the Charcoal Club, a short-lived organization, which lasted from early spring to early autumn of 1893. Dissatisfied with the teaching methods and restricted environment of the Pennsylvania Academy, John Sloan and Joseph Laub organized the Club as an alternative space in which to work. The Charcoal Club met for three nightly sessions a week during which the members, local Philadelphia newspapermen and former students of the Pennsylvania Academy, sketched and painted from the nude model. On Monday evenings Sloan and Robert Henri would provide critiques of the members' work. Membership dues were two dollars a month, half what was charged at the Pennsylvania Academy.

The attractive price and the stimulating environment added to the club's success.

At the height of its popularity, the group counted 38 members including Shinn, Joe Laub, Glackens, Edward Davis (father of the artist Stuart Davis) and Frederic Gruger. Shinn may have learned about the Charcoal Club while working at the *Press* where Glackens and Davis were on staff. Glackens had recently joined the *Press* after spending a year at the Philadelphia *Record*, and Davis was the paper's art director.[18] For Shinn, the Charcoal Club afforded both art training and, perhaps more importantly, an introduction to some of the artists with whom he would later exhibit as The Eight. Art historian Mahonri Sharp Young colorfully expressed the significance of the Charcoal Club, stating "The Club only ran through the summer, but the great Philadelphia gang was formed at this time, with Henri at the head, Sloan at the shoulder, and Glackens, Luks, and Shinn right behind. This was the start of the Eight."[19] Despite the enthusiasm of the members, by the summer months attendance for the Charcoal Club began to dwindle. The heat combined with the depression of 1893 resulted in the demise of the Club in mid-September. In the fall, former students returned to the Academy accompanied by one of its newest members, Everett Shinn, whose name first appears in the School Register on October 13, 1893.

The curriculum at the Pennsylvania Academy during Shinn's tenure was rigidly academic. Beginning students started with the antique class, and only after lengthy sessions of drawing from the antique cast, did he or she progress to the life class; there was no drawing from the nude. Although he may have been disappointed with the tedium of drawing from the antique, the Academy did afford him the opportunity to study with some the nation's most talented teachers, most notably Thomas Anshutz. Anshutz, who from 1875 to 1880 had been a student of Thomas Eakins, took over many of his former teacher's classes at the Academy after Eakins's dismissal. He carried out many of Eakins's precepts and continued his emphasis on the human figure.

Shinn divided his time working the graveyard shift at the *Press* and attending the Pennsylvania Academy during the day. At the time of his enrollment, Sloan and Glackens had been attending the Academy for two years. Both men first registered in the Academy's antique class in October 1891 and by April of 1892, had graduated to the life class. Also studying at the Academy was Florence Scovel, a talented young artist, who like Shinn was from New Jersey.[20] Shinn began a courtship with Florence Scovel, or "Flossie" as friends knew her, and the two were married in 1898.

Shinn, Glackens and Sloan found the academic teaching style of the Academy stifling, but Henri encouraged them to continue their studies. Shinn, however, believed that he learned very little at the Academy and later claimed:

> All the time spent at the Academy was only as a club house and with no interest in the institution itself. Other people worked and went to class but we never did. Most of our time was spent in the "Dissecting Room" discussing everything but art with a bottle lowered out of the window on a rope so we could bring in beer.[21]

At the Pennsylvania Academy friendships forged amongst members of the Charcoal Club were strengthened. The Club's spirit experienced an afterlife in the form of weekly open house meetings in Henri's studio at 806 Walnut Street. The gatherings initially took place on Thursday evenings, but the day was later changed to Tuesday. During these sessions Henri led the group of Academy students and young illustrators in a range of discussions. Sloan was a devoted member of the Tuesday night sessions; other regulars included Charles Grafly, James Preston, F. R. Gruger, Edward Redfield, and Hugh Breckenridge. Shinn and Luks often attended, although the hard-drinking Luks tended to find Henri's discourses a bit too long-winded.[22] A natural speaker, Henri provided impassioned discourses on painting, music, and literature. The newspapermen were encouraged to study the work of Edouard Manet, Francisco

Goya, Diego Velasquez, Edgar Degas, and to read William Morris's *Talks on Art* and George Moore's *Modern Painting*. In her Doctoral dissertation on the illustrations of Shinn and Luks, Nina Kasanof notes that the artists at Henri's studio gatherings admired and were influenced by the graphic artists Honoré Daumier, Gavarni (Sulpice Guillaume Chevalier), Théophile Steinlen, Jean-Louis Forain, Walter Crane, John Leech, Charles Keene, and George du Maurier.[23] Henri inspired his listeners and urged them to paint the life with which they had become so familiar as newspaper illustrators. As Sloan recalled, "It was Robert Henri who set me to painting seriously; without his inspiring friendship and guidance I probably might never have thought of it at all."[24]

In addition to providing a nucleus for theoretical discussions, 806 Walnut also afforded a gathering place for the group's social life. Evening entertainment included dinner, music and amateur performances in which almost everyone participated. Shinn made his acting debut in the most well known of the group's performances, *Twillbe*, a satire based on George du Maurier's best selling novel, *Trilby*. Henri played Svengali and Shinn was cast in the role of the American expatriate James McNails Whiskers. During the day, Shinn recalled that the group would "haunt the art galleries and study the work of current illustrators."[25] Glackens introduced them

to the work of Keene and Du Maurier, and taught them to appreciate the style of Thomas Eakins and Winslow Homer.[26]

In many ways it seems that Henri's gatherings provided a more satisfying education than that offered at the Pennsylvania Academy. Despite the school's prestigious faculty and the benefits of formal instruction, Shinn's tenure at the Academy was of short duration. According to the Academy's register books, Shinn only enrolled for four terms, the first beginning on October 13th, 1893 and second on January 31, 1894, the third October 13, 1894 and the last January 31, 1895. By the 1895–1896 term, his name is no longer on the register.[27] The brevity of Shinn's attendance may be partially attributed to his temperament and his impatience with formal education. Moreover, as Shinn found his job on the *Press* more rewarding and educational than the classes he was attending, it does not seem that it was a difficult decision for him to leave the Academy.

Life as a New York City Illustrator

At the end 1897, Shinn was lured away from the Philadelphia newspapers by an offer to work as an illustrator at the New York *World* for a two-dollar pay increase. Luks had been the first of the group to move to New York after his return from Cuba. In April of 1896, Luks who had begun work at the New York *World* encouraged his friends to follow suit. By the end of the year Glackens joined Luks in New York where he worked briefly at the *World* before accepting an offer from its archrival, the New York *Herald*. When Shinn arrived in New York, Luks and Glackens were already rooming together so Shinn took a flat alone.[28] Other illustrators including Alden March and Edward Davis also left Philadelphia for New York newspapers. Of the group, Sloan was the last to leave; though he made a tentative effort to relocate in 1898, he returned to Philadelphia a few months later and did not permanently settle in New York until 1904.

New York at the time of Shinn's arrival was a city in the process of great transition. During the 19th century the Old Dutch City had metamorphized into the country's largest city. In 1898, when the five boroughs combined to form Greater New York, the city's population nearly doubled. Beginning downtown at the tip of Manhattan, the city's northern boundaries were constantly redefined as

building and development expanded rapidly uptown. Newly constructed plazas, parks, theaters, restaurants and other public buildings transformed the landscape. During the last quarter of the century the city witnessed the creation of elaborate and eclectic private mansions modeled on English castles and Renaissance palazzos.

This was the bustling, constantly changing kaleidoscope of a city in which Shinn hoped to establish himself. Despite his years in Philadelphia, he was still a relatively inexperienced young man from a small town and the city's magnitude must have been a little over-whelming. Shinn recalled his hesitancy as he approached New York City from the Hoboken Ferry: "An awareness of some trap I had set for myself brought panic and despair…. Above me glittered a frozen storm of stars, an incandescent glow from the cities [sic] towers hung from the sky…. Could anyone live in peace under that blazing canopy? Could I concentrate in its muffled roar? Would my hand be steady for my work? I had come to try."[29]

On January 26, 1898 Shinn married Florence Scovel (Flossie) in Philadelphia where she was then living.[30] After the wedding Flossie joined Shinn in New York moving into his residence at 145 East 21st Street. In 1900 the couple moved to 122 East 19th Street, before finding a permanent residence in 1902 in a townhouse on 112 Waverly Place just off Washington Square where they would remain until their divorce in 1912.

At the beginning of 1899, Shinn left the art department of the New York *World* for the more independent life of the magazines. At the end of the century newspapers were turning to photo-reproduction and many artist-reporters felt that their profession was threatened by the new technology. Although it would still be about twenty years before photography replaced illustration, newspaper artists were looking for ways to diversify. Magazines welcomed the illustrator and afforded a more relaxed environment in which to work. *Century Magazine*, *Scribner's Magazine*, and *Harper's Weekly* were considered genteel journals that catered to a middle-class audience who appreciated fiction and other types of "subjective" writing that were still the province of illustration.

In January 1899, Shinn accepted a job as art editor for *Ainslee's Magazine*, a position that proved very advantageous. During his tenure with the journal he illustrated numerous articles and assisted his friends Sloan, Glackens, William Buckland and James Preston to secure work with the magazine. Flossie was also an active contributor, whose illustrations were included in almost every issue of *Ainslee's Magazine* during 1899. In addition to *Ainslee's Magazine*, Flossie's work appeared in periodicals such as *Life*, *Truth*, and *Century Magazine*. Her success as an illustrator made a significant

impact on the household income, and while they were married Shinn was able to limit substantially his magazine illustration. He did continue to work for a few periodicals and in 1906, he contributed 20 drawings for the novel *Frederique* by Charles Paul de Kock, a project he shared with Glackens, Luks, Sloan, James Preston, and Frederick R. Gruger.[31] In 1913, following his divorce from Flossie, Shinn resumed accepting numerous illustration commissions.

Picturing New York City

Although Shinn would eventually become as equally well known for his theater pictures as for his city scenes, from 1898 until his trip to Europe in 1900, the metropolitan streets were his primary subject. In selecting this theme he was joining a host of other artists, past and present, who pictured New York City. Beginning in the 19th century, Manhattan captured the imagination of many artists, who were preoccupied with the city's modernity and uniqueness.[32] The floods of people that poured into the city from foreign countries and rural parts of the United States, necessitated the creation of city infrastructure — new buildings were constructed, parks laid out and transportation systems developed. As residents marveled at the construction of new edifices, the city's rapid changes became the topic of scores of articles, which both lauded and scorned the rapid developments. Like the writers of essays on New York City, photographers and painters who rendered the metropolis both celebrated the changes as progress and lamented the disappearance of old New York.

The American Impressionists were the first group of painters to focus so intensely on New York City. In paintings influenced by French artists such as Claude Monet and Camille Pissarro, American Impressionists presented a positive view of New York's fashionable avenues, gleaming bridges, and verdant parks. It was the city itself, not its denizens that attracted the attention of these artists. As William H. Gerdts notes in his book *Impressionist New York*, the inhabitants of the city "were relatively incidental to the American Impressionists proper."[33] The artists often employed a high vantage point, reducing the pedestrians to barely visible dabs of paint.

When New Yorkers do make appearances, they are generally representative of the patrician class and are pictured in decorous environments. The image of Central Park presented in William Merritt Chase's *Lake for Miniature Sailboats, Central Park* (c. 1890; Collection of Mr. and Mrs. Peter G. Terian, New York) is a clean, garden-like space where well-behaved upper-middle-class children play with sailboats. Fashionable avenues are represented in Childe Hassam's paintings, *Fifth Avenue and Madison Square* (1891; Thyssen-Bornemisza Museum, Madrid) and *Spring Morning*, (c. 1890/91; Private Collection), which bespeak the elegance of turn-of-the-century New York. In these pictures fashionably dressed women stroll down clean well-kept streets or step into waiting carriages. Although Hassam did occasionally paint the working class, for the most part his interpretations of the city are positive, avoiding any sense of suffering or urban squalor.

Like the American Impressionists, the work of the Ashcan artists also has antecedents in the work of the French Impressionists. Although the Ashcan artists have traditionally been considered the antithesis of the Impressionists, Gerdts has argued that the Ashcan School may be seen as a continuation of the figurative Impressionists.[34] In the United States during the last quarter of the 20th century, Impressionism came to be associated with Monet and characterized by landscapes. The grittier side of Impressionism, that which dealt with the tougher side of modern life such as workers, commerce, and industrialization, was rejected by critics and patrons. In 1886 when Durand-Ruel Galleries sent the first major exhibition of French Impressionist work to New York a reviewer stated:

> The complex problems of human life which make the figurative subjects so terrible in their pessimism and seem to fill the air with cries of uneasy souls, have no part in the landscapes. These are wholly

lovely with the loveliness of repose and the tenderness of charity. They are full of heavenly calm.[35]

It is not surprising that Shinn, Luks, Glackens and Sloan became chroniclers of the urban scene. During their student days in Philadelphia, Henri had encouraged the newspaper artists to portray the metropolitan themes they knew so well from illustration and from everyday life.[36]

In contrast to the American Impressionists' genteel treatment of the city, Shinn and his fellow Ashcan artists focused on a broader perspective of city life. Rather than the look of the city itself — e.g., its buildings and bridges—they were concerned with New York's inhabitants. Immigrants, newsboys, and shop girls were depicted at street level. The city's public spaces became a kind of stage where one's behaviors were observed, studied, and recorded. As Rebecca Zurier has noted in regard to the Ashcan artists, "All six artists were newcomers to the city, and their work reveals experiences common to most New Yorkers at the time: The challenge of making sense out of encounters with strangers in a city of unprecedented scale and growth."[37]

Taking Zurier's statement as a point of departure, I would argue that part of the significance of Shinn's early work and the reason that it was so successful so early in his career was that it offered examples of city life that helped people clarify their own roles in the burgeoning cul-

ture of New York City. By portraying recognizable New York landmarks and establishments — the Washington Arch, the Dewey Arch, Gramercy Park, and Delmonico's — Shinn presented the city in a format that the 19th century audience would have immediately recognized — that of being on a city tour. The structure was a stock convention at the time and used in the numerous books on the city (see, for example, *Impressions and Experiences* by William Dean Howells). However, as has been discussed above, the Ashcan artists were not merely interested in the appearance of the city but the people who occupied it. In Shinn's pictures the recognizable landmark is often shown off to the side or obliquely, the real subject of the work is the people who occupy the space surrounding structure. Significantly, the figures in Shinn's pictures are often shown trudging through snow or making their way down crowded city streets. Sometimes the people seem to struggle with their situation presenting conditions with which New Yorkers could empathize. Thus pictures may have also served to help a diverse population form bonds through common experience.

In *City People: The Rise of Modern City Culture in Nineteenth-Century America*, historian Gunter Barth describes the formation of an urban identity as it occurred in the United States during late 19th century. He writes:

Most people accepted the heterogeneity of their world as an integral component of their lives…. To give and take of daily chores, the mingling of people in crowded streets, in parks and theaters, shops and factories, exposed them to a multitude of different influences. Over the years these encounters eroded old loyalties. From the chaos emerged the experience of living with the various elements of a new, diverse culture. This awareness of others produced an urban identity that stamped members of heterogeneous groups generally as city people.[38]

Barth argues that the new social and economic institutions of the apartment house, the metropolitan press, the department store, the baseball park, and the vaudeville stage facilitated the forging of a collective experience by affording a means to a modern urban identity. This thesis is relevant to an understanding of the work of Shinn both in the context of his city scenes and specifically, as we will see, in his pictures of the vaudeville stage. Shinn selected urban spaces where people likely would have recognized themselves as active spectators in an ongoing dialogue between themselves and the metropolitan environment. It this context Shinn's works were not only commercially successful, they were sociologically meaningful.

A Modern Master of Pastel

Shinn is a master of pastel; he knows thoroughly both the possibilities and the limitations of his medium. The material is never strained in endeavoring to get too much out of it; and if technically his pastels are great achievements, pictorially they are also.

— A. E. GALLATIN, "Studio Talk," *International Studio* 30 (November 1906): 86.

Shinn's great productivity as a pastel painter begins in 1899.[39] Until 1901, Shinn worked almost exclusively in pastel and even after he began to experiment with oil, pastel remained a favorite medium. By the late 1890s, pastel had experienced a general revival and American taste for the medium had broadened. Factors contributing to the revival of pastel include the exhibition of 289 works by European Impressionists, which opened at the American Art Galleries in New York on April 9, 1886. Sent by the French gallery Durand-Ruel to New York, the exhibition, which included 73 pastels and watercolors, did much to elevate the status of pastel. Moreover, the success of artists such as James McNeill Whistler and Giuseppe de Nittis enhanced the reputation of pastel painting as did a series of exhibitions organized by the Society of Painters in Pastel beginning in 1884 and continuing in 1888, 1889 and 1890.[40]

What the public was not accustomed to, however, was Shinn's unusual use of the medium.[41] Works in pastel as treated by practitioners such as Whistler or Thomas Wilmer Dewing were delicate, emphasizing soft color harmonies and understated elegance. The subjects portrayed, for example, gentle landscapes, lovely women and vases of flowers, followed the tastes of genteel society. Shinn's pastels were another thing entirely. Two of his earliest pastels, *Fire Scene* (1899; Yale University Art Gallery)[42] and *Woman at the Chicken Coop* (1899; Private Collection; PLATE 1) demonstrate not only a departure in subject matter from the conventional treatment of pastel, but also a radically different technique. In *Fire Scene* the medium is used to render dilapidated buildings with grimy facades and broken shutters articulated in rapid, vigorously applied stokes of pastel. *Woman at the Chicken Coop*, unusual for Shinn as it departs from his typical urban subject matter, portrays a woman working in a farmyard rather than posed in an elegant setting. The emphasis on black and white with the addition of a few bright colors is characteristic of Shinn's early pastels.

Shinn's images of modern life, which required a sense of immediacy and spontaneity, lent themselves well to rendering in pastel.[43] He may also have appreciated the way pastel was compatible with other mediums. Although he produced many pure pastels, several works combined pastel with watercolor and gouache, and occasionally, pastel over a monotype print (for example, *Circus* [1906; The Metropolitan Museum of Art]).

Stormy Weather

Many of Shinn's most original pastels of New York are distinguished by the skillful way they portray the city in inclement weather. Throughout his career, Shinn was to exploit the aesthetic possibilities of rain and snow, feeling that individuals straining against the elements added pictorial interest to what might otherwise become static urban views. Frequently he would depict the same scene, for example Washington Square, under varying weather conditions and at different times of day. Of the possible seasonal conditions under which to portray the city, Shinn's favorite was New York veiled in snow. The snowstorm was particularly appropriate for New York City, which in 1888 and 1899 had experienced crippling blizzards. In addition to the numerous pictures Shinn painted of actual snowstorms, he also would introduce snow into scenes where none had previously existed. In his autobiography Shinn recounted an incident when his wife was ill. He recalled, "She asked me to make a city street packed with snow. I made one of Gramercy Park from our window. It was placed at the foot of her bed. It made her feel cool. Previously I made snow scenes in summer and sticky hot streets in winter."[44]

"New York by Night"

Many of Shinn's early pastels were conceived as illustrations for a book he began preparing around 1899 called "New York by Night."[45] According to Shinn, the book was to be composed of "a set of colored pictures.... The book opened on the close of any day of toil in the city, following every activity of the night until it finished its cycle of comedy and drama on Park Row and its line of newspaper buildings where trucks spread out to stands and stations the news in another dawn."[46] Not only was the book to illustrate nightlife in New York, but the format would underscore the city's extreme contrasts. Shinn described the book as: "75 pages of alternative gaiety and drabness — a Bowery restaurant — hunger inside and out...The opposite page, old Delmonico's blazing facade — carriages, hansoms. No need to picture the interior...champagne, truffles.[47]

"New York by Night" was part of a continuing tradition of illustrated articles, lectures and books on the city.[48] The best known of the genre was the exposé *How The Other Half Lives*, 1890, by the Danish-American Jacob Riis.[49] The book, which was crucial in stimulating social reform and helping to eliminate the horrendous living conditions on the Lower East Side, also fed the public's curiosity about life in the tenements. Even before Riis's publication, the public was familiar with books that described the diversity of city life, particularly those that divided New York into distinct halves. The Reverend Matthew Hale Smith's *Sunshine and Shadow in New York* and James D. McCabe's *Lights and Shadows of New York Life* exaggerate the polarities between high life and low life — splendor is contrasted with wretchedness, the palaces of merchant princes with dens of infamy and crime.[50] In this diverse environment, which Henry James referred to as *a pot au feu,* individuals wondered and speculated about one another.[51] When they could, they stared at each other in the street. Some more adventurous souls followed the guidebooks into the "foreign" territory of the Lower East Side. Most people, however, relied upon essays by realist writers such as William Dean Howells or pictures by artists like Shinn to provide them with a way to see and make sense of the diverse city.

Shinn and Howells first met on March 5, 1900 when Jeanette Gilder, editor of *The Critic*, sent the artist to draw Howells for the magazine. From this initial encounter, the two men formed a friendship and Howells became a great admirer of Shinn's work.[52] When Shinn went to enlist Howells's interest in "New York by Night," the author was enthusiastic and offered to write a running commentary through the pages.[53] Unfortunately, if the commentary was ever written, it is now unlocated.

As late as 1959, 35 of the pastels for "New York by Night" were still together and the group was exhibited at The Henry

Clay Frick Fine-Arts Department in Pittsburgh. Subsequently, the pictures were separated, making it almost impossible to reassemble the book.[54] We can, however, identify two works with certainty and can be reasonably confident about the attribution of several others. *Madison Square* (1899; Saint Louis Art Museum) was most likely intended as the book's cover or title page as it bears "Night York by Night" across its top margin. *Tenements at Hester Street* (1900; FIG. 1) can also be assigned with certainty to "Night York by Night." Using loose sketchy brushwork, Shinn employs watercolor and gouache to portray a hot night on the Lower East Side. In order to escape the oppressive heat of overcrowded and poorly ventilated apartments, residents have camped out on roofs. The tenement dwellers seem to have become de-humanized by their situation. One individual hangs his head and arms limply out the window; another is shown in his undershirt indecorously sprawled on the fire escape. Although Shinn continually professed that he had no interest in social reform, his pictures nevertheless managed to serve a social good. Referring to this work Shinn later wrote:

> Several years ago — over forty at any rate, I was showing Mrs. J. Pierpont Morgan and her secretary an elaborate new book I was preparing for Harper's [sic] Brothers entitled 'New York by Night'....One particular drawing gave Mrs. Morgan much concern:

Squalid tenements, children huddled in rags on fire-escapes, families side by side on a caved-in roof…. Mrs. Morgan questioned my drawing as representing the truth. Truth, but understated — as odor could not be given unless I dropped my drawing in refuse. A week later, Mrs. Morgan's secretary told me that Mrs. Morgan had opened a haven for those unfortunate souls on the lower East Side. I had no intention or hope for this happening — it so happened that one who could help saw the drawings. That drawing is now in the Philips Memorial.[55]

The pastels created for "Night York by Night" provide an excellent example of

[FIG. 1] *Tenements at Hester Street*, 1900
Watercolor, gouache, and ink on paper
8¼ x 13 inches
The Phillips Collection, Washington, D.C.

Shinn's fascination, even at this early date, with vastly divergent types of public spaces that distinguished turn-of-the-century Manhattan. Shinn continued to work on the project after his return from Europe in the fall of 1900. The post-1900 pictures are distinguished by their portrayal of dramatic effects of light resulting from fireworks and fires. In all, Shinn completed 36 pastels for the project and tried to publish the book several times, even registering for a copyright at the Library of Congress on February 12, 1900. However, the book never came to fruition and Shinn eventually exhibited the works at galleries, greatly contributing to the body of his early work.[56]

The Public Space (1898–1900)

Shinn's fascination with the spectacle of modern life is apparent in his earliest renderings of the public spaces of New York, which portray an array of subjects often contrasting genteel New York with its rougher "other half." The rendering of the elegant figures in *Park Scene* (c. 1899; PLATE 4) might seem to come from another world when placed side by side on a gallery wall with a picture of Lower Manhattan shown in *Park Row, Fruit Vendors* (c. 1899; PLATE 9). However, both images represent the public space emphasizing not just the subject's location in New York, but how it functioned as a site of cultural exchange. At a time when wealth was being consolidated and the city's elite were able to withdraw into the private spaces of clubs and mansions, the urban spaces of the streets, parks, and squares provided points of interclass contact.[57] Shinn wandered the city streets as an urban *flâneur* observing and recording a multifaceted vision of New York. His record book lists locations such as Union Square, Washington Square, Madison Square, Broadway and 23rd Street, the docks, and Park Row. The mixing of people in public spaces was a salient issue during the last decades of the 19th century. As historian Robert Snyder explains:

> The spatial organization of New York reflected the growing diversity and complexity of its commercial, social, and recreational activities.

The most intense cultural commerce took place in and around the major axes or squares of the city, and the central focus made its way north along Broadway from City Hall Park in the 1840s and 1850s to Times Square by about 1910. By the 1890s, Madison Square had become the focus of the city's life, serving briefly as its public center.[58]

Madison Square Park

The Shinns' residence at 145 East 21st Street was located only a few blocks from Madison Square Park, which in the late 1890s was one of the city's busiest and most glamorous squares. It was also one of the city's newest squares; the city acquired the land in 1837 and developed the area a few years later. The square's position as an aristocratic district was secured in 1853 when the Presbyterian Church was constructed at Madison Avenue and East 24th Street. The construction of the church was followed by the building of several luxury hotels and fashionable residences, which immediately transported a sense of majesty and elegance to the area. In the 1870s, the square also became a site of urban entertainment. P. T. Barnum's Roman Hippodrome opened in 1871 and in 1879 the first Madison Square Garden was inaugurated. In June of 1890 the original Madison Square Garden was replaced by a second version, a spectacular building designed by Stanford White. Built at a cost of $3,000,000, it was the largest building in the United States devoted solely to amusements. Inside Madison Square Garden one could indulge in horse and dog shows, circuses, and sports events. During the summer months the roof garden was devoted to vaudeville performances. The exterior of the building was finished in buff brick and tile and rising up into the air was the building's spectacular tower crowned by Saint-Gaudens's gilded figure of Diana. Other notable sites of the square included Café Martin, which until 1897 had been the site of the glamorous dining establishment Delmonico's.[59]

Not only did the square offer an impressive confluence of hostelries, private residences, religious institutions, and leisure activities, but the area was also literally at the crossroads of the city's two major arteries, Broadway and Fifth Avenue. The intersection is represented in the pastel *A Rainy Day in Madison Square* (1898; PLATE 2), which features a bustling array of carriages, streetcars and pedestrians. The square was referred to as New York's equivalent to the Place de la Concorde.[60] As one writer admiringly described the location:

> In the very heart of the metropolis of the New World is Madison Square; and in all New York there is no other one place so completely identified with the growth of the

city as this beautiful pleasance. Even more than this may be said, for it is doubtful if there is any place in the world where the *fin de siècle* civilization in the fullest development can be seen to greater advantage than in this very Madison Square. It has all the gayety and brightness of the famous Place de la Concorde in Paris, without its sad reminiscences. Like Trafalgar Square in London, it has a memorial to a nation's naval hero…. The history of Madison Square is indeed the history of New York city itself.[61]

For Shinn, Madison Square afforded a spectacle of visual material from which he created several dazzling pastels. This was genteel New York and Shinn took advantage of the location to depict the square's fashionably dressed men and women and the fine establishments. The area's prominence is reaffirmed by an 1899 Baedeker's guide, which advises, "one should obtain good accommodation in the best neighborhood (e.g. near Madison Sq.)."[62] While he occasionally depicted other squares, for example Washington Square, between 1898 and 1901 Madison Square was the square he most frequently represented. The square is shown from different angles, under various weather conditions, and despite its glamorous location, as a locus for different types of people.

Park Scene (1899; PLATE 4), arguably Shinn's most gracious depiction of a city park, is most likely the pastel referred to in Shinn's record book as *Madison Square (Thaw)*. The viewer is led into the picture by a broad sweep of pavement. The pastel's color harmonies are limited to a palette of blacks, grays and whites with touches of red. Walking toward the viewer, on a path shiny with melted snow, is an elegantly dressed couple — he in a top hat and long black evening coat and she in a smart looking dress with a fur collar and muff. Perhaps they have just come from one of the fine restaurants or hotels on the square and are now taking a stroll through the park. In any event, a contemporary viewer would likely have viewed them as a spectacle of uptown elegance, to be looked upon as an example of the latest in fashionable clothing and respectable deportment.

That Shinn showed *Madison Square (Thaw)* numerous times in exhibitions critical to the launching of his career suggests the high regard he had for the work. It was amongst a group of pastels Shinn submitted (unsuccessfully) to the Society of American Artists for exhibition from March 25 to April 29, 1899.[63] The pastel made its public debut at the Association of Allied Artists from April 10 to 15, 1899. It was amongst the five paintings exhibited at the home of Elsie de Wolfe, which caught the eye of Stanford White, and it was shown in Shinn's first large one-man show at Boussod, Valadon & Co., which then traveled to the Pennsylvania Academy. In January 1901, *Madison Square (Thaw)* and *Madison Square Cabs* were lent to a Miss Rhett who resided at 122 East 34th Street. Purchased by J.P. Morgan for Miss Rhett, the picture was then lent by its new owner to Shinn's exhibition at J. Eastman Chase's Gallery[64] where it drew encomiums from a critic:

> Madison Square (Thaw) number 4, is good, too, representing a gray black asphalt walk dark and shining from the snow which has newly melted away. There is dingy whitey gray snow, to each side of the walk. In the middle distance one can catch site of furtive little figures away and beyond the trees. Farther yet are typical sky scrapers, while down the walk come two quite "swell" figures done with very considerable skill and dash.[65]

In *Hansom Cabs in Snow* (c. 1899; PLATE 3), the vantage point is from the west side of the square looking across the broad expanse of Fifth Avenue to Madison Square Park.[66] In the middle-ground two figures make their way across the street perhaps toward the line of hansom cabs that front the park. In the background, the park itself is veiled in an atmospheric haze.[67] The palette is limited to white and varying shades of chocolate browns highlighted by dabs of yellow to express the shimmering light emanating from the windows on the far side of the square.

A New York audience would have immediately recognized the view of Madison Square presented in this pastel by the identifiable landmarks. In the background to the left one can make out the spire of the Madison Square Presbyterian Church at the corner of Madison Avenue and 24th Street. The large building to the right of it was the first Metropolitan Life Insurance building on 23rd Street and Madison Avenue. Also, while not unique to Madison Square, the picturesque line of hansom cabs was associated with the park and featured in the work of other artists (e.g., Childe Hassam) and mentioned in articles about the area. In "Up-Town in New York," the author Jesse Lynch Williams observes, "But when Madison Square is reached you have come to one of the Places of New York. It is the picture that so many confirmed New Yorkers see when homesick…a soft purple light under the branches in the park, a long decorative row of cabs waiting for 'fares;' over toward the statue of Farragut, and lithe New York women wearing clothes as they alone know how to wear them, crossing Fifth Avenue at Twenty-third street."[68] When the pastel was shown in the exhibition at Boussod, Valadon & Co. in 1900 it was singled out by a reviewer as being "Among the best of the street scenes."[69]

Hansom Cabs in Snow relates to a similar picture, *A Rainy Day in Madison Square* (1898; PLATE 2). The vantage point is from the southwest side of the square looking across the broad expanse of Fifth Avenue. At the right in the background are the buildings lining 23rd Street while in the background at the left one can clearly make out the Presbyterian Church and the Metropolitan Life Insurance building. The cursory manner of pastel treatment suggests Shinn's rapid technique and effectively captures the profusion of vehicles and pedestrians that vied for space at one of the city's busiest crossroads. In addition to the hansom cabs shown traveling both up and down Fifth Avenue, Shinn has included the Fifth Avenue horse drawn bus, which not only adds a picturesque detail, but also emphasizes the variety of visual display afforded by the square.[70]

Some of Shinn's most dynamic and interesting views of Madison Square are the ones that include the Dewey Arch. To celebrate Admiral George Dewey's victory over the Spanish forces at Manila Bay on May 1, 1898 during the Spanish American War, the City of New York threw a gala reception. The festivities continued from September 27th to the 30th and included troop maneuvers, parades and the dedication of the triumphal Dewey Arch. Although only a temporary structure built in two months of staff (plaster reinforced with hay or burlap), the arch was considered a *tour de force* of architectural and sculptural achievement. Designed by the architect Charles R. Lamb, it was modeled on the Arch of Titus in Rome. The abundant sculptural decoration was the responsi-

bility of the sculptor Frederic Wellington Ruckstuhl. Sculptors employed included well-known names such as Daniel Chester French, Karl Bitter, Charles Niehaus, J. Q. A. Ward, Isidore Conti, George Bissel and Herbert Adams.[71]

The location of the arch at the junction of Fifth Avenue and Broadway at Madison Square is a testament to the importance of the square. As a contemporary writer noted:

> Even before the route of the parade was determined, it was evident that it would pass this point; it was a spot so nearly central in the life of the busy city as to be for all practical purposes the real center; and it afforded a larger open area than could elsewhere be had without considerably diminishing the accessibility to the arch. Moreover, the junction of the two principal thoroughfares of the metropolis formed here a focal point of special importance. All things considered, therefore, Madison Square seemed not only the most suitable place for the arch, but really the only one available.[72]

The arch's placement on Fifth Avenue aligned it with the Washington Square Arch thus establishing a triumphal corridor. Though efforts were begun to make the arch a permanent structure, the plan was abandoned after Dewey failed to gain the Democratic presidential nomination, his popularity having been eclipsed by that of Theodore Roosevelt. The Dewey Arch was dismantled in December 1900, but testaments to its splendor remain in photographs and paintings. Both Childe Hassam and the French artist Jean-Francois Raffaëlli created views of the arch from similar perspectives looking north up Fifth Avenue. In these depictions the arch, prominently featured, gleaming white and parallel to the picture plane, is clearly the center of attention.[73]

Shinn portrayed the Dewey Arch at least three times in *Madison Square and the Dewey Arch: Cross Streets of New York* (1899; Location Unknown), *Madison Square, Dewey Arch* (1899; PLATE 5), and *The Dewey Arch, Madison Square* (1899; Private Collection). In contrast to Hassam's and Raffaëlli's more conventional views of the arch, Shinn's depictions of the subject depart significantly from the typical viewpoint. In Shinn's representations, the arch, though clearly recognizable, is shown as a background element rather than the main subject. Emphasis is placed instead on the weather conditions and the people in the park.

In *Madison Square, Dewey Arch* the viewer is led into the park by a broad sweeping path. In contrast to the well-dressed figures that appear in *Park Scene*, here the leading protagonists are a group of working-class men. With their bowler hats, simple brown coats, and lunch pails, they form a stark contrast to the

elaborate arch in the background. The pastel is unusual as it shows men who are workers, but who are not currently engaged in work, wandering through what was generally considered one of the city's more refined public spaces. It was not that workers did not also share places like Madison Square, but rarely were they made the focal point in representations of them. By highlighting these men, Shinn seems to be emphasizing the ability of the public square to function as a democratic space open to all social and economic classes and affording the possibility of encounters between them.

Moving through the City: Transportation

The inhabitants of New York City were also brought together by Manhattan's public transportation system. The city's extraordinary population growth — 3,437,000 people by 1900[74] — resulted in densely packed city streets teaming with buses, trolleys, horse carts and pedestrians. For Shinn, the city's thoroughfares provided a constant stream of picturesque activity — people are frequently depicted walking or trudging through snow while a metropolitan bus or El train passes by. Shinn's pictures of New York's complex network of transportation in a manner of speaking move the viewer through the city.

At the turn of the century the elevated railroad, or the "El" as it was commonly called, was considered the modern and fashionable way to travel. Established in 1867, the El was an immediate success and by 1899 was utilized by two hundred million passengers annually.[75] Not only was it almost twice as fast as private hackney cabs and hansom carriages, but at five cents a ride it was substantially cheaper than the hackney carriages which charged one dollar just for the first mile.[76] For Shinn the great appeal of the El was most likely the way it brought together such a diverse range of people. To a greater degree than even the city streets, the El concentrated different social classes, ethnic types and age groups in a compact space. Unlike European trains, which separated passengers into different classes depending on the price of the ticket, the El had no such divisions. The co-mingling of rich and poor that occurred on the El was frequently noted by English visitors and writers such as William Dean Howells, who offered the following appraisal of the El through the eyes of the character Basil March:

> He found the variety of people in the car as unfailingly entertaining as ever. He rather preferred the East Side to the West Side lines, because they offered more nationalities, characters and conditions for inspection. They draw not only from the uptown American region,

but from all the vast hive of populations swarming between them and the East River.[77]

In *Cooper Square* (c. 1900–1908; PLATE 8) the El is shown in the background acting as a barrier dividing the buildings on the east side of Third Avenue from the open space of Cooper Square. Emphasizing the wide range of people who congregated near El stops, the pastel features a large foreground plane upon which several vignettes are being played out. In the background a horse cart lumbers through the snow while at the right two boys are playing. The points of greatest interest, however, are the three couples that form points of a triangle. The viewer's eye first moves back in space to the couple in the background center whose forward movement pulls us back toward the edge of the picture plane. Here two couples, one on the right and one on the left, struggle to negotiate the treacherous puddles formed by melting snow. The couple on the left is more fashionably dressed than the modestly garbed pair on the right, underscoring the mix of social classes that intersected in the square. Crossroads such as these provided the opportunity for observing others unlike oneself. Indeed the man on the left has turned to stare at the other couple whose fine clothing and perhaps upper-class demeanor provided its own urban spectacle. *Cooper Square* is related to a pastel titled *A Rainy Day at Cooper*

Square (1935; The Metropolitan Museum of Art), which features the same location but with different foreground figures.

To the degree that Shinn's pictures of the El were considered images of modern transportation, his depictions of the metropolitan omnibuses were recognized as looking back to an old-fashioned mode of travel. The omnibuses were actually horse-pulled stagecoaches painted red, white and blue and popular all over downtown. Displaced by the introduction of the streetcar, the buses were relegated first to Broadway, then to Fifth Avenue where by the 1890s they had become quaint symbols of elegant old New York and tourist attractions.[78] Shinn depicted the metropolitan bus at least three times in *Fifth Avenue Coach, Winter* (c. 1899; The Montclair Art Museum), *Horsedrawn Bus* (1899; PLATE 6) and *Fifth Avenue* (c. 1899; PLATE 7).[79] All three pastels portray the stage in the midst of a violent snowstorm. The vivid imagery was most likely inspired by an actual storm that began on February 11, 1899 and paralyzed the city for four days. On February 14, 1899 the *New York Times* reported:

> One of the severest snowstorms that have ever visited New York struck the city Sunday night and raged all day yesterday. Except for the memorable blizzard of 1888, no combination of the elements within recent memory has wrought such mischief. Traffic in the city and in all directions was brought almost to a standstill…. The price of coal went up. One-tenth of the city's population had no gas for fuel or lighting because of frozen pipes.[80]

The intensity of such a storm is manifest in *Horsedrawn Bus* (1899; PLATE 6) in which Shinn, using rapid, vigorous strokes of pastel, effectively conveys the extreme weather conditions. The horsedrawn bus has stopped to allow passengers on and off. At the far right, a female who has just disembarked can be seen struggling with her umbrella. Behind her, another passenger emerges from the back of the bus. Rendered in a restrained palette of whites and blacks, the pastel is enlivened by effectively placed passages of red and blue on the bus and highlights of yellow pastel indicating the welcoming lights of an apartment building. Shinn's rapid application of dense pastel in the wide foreground plane effectively conveys the sense of a snow-rutted street, while in the background the more feathery treatment of the medium creates the sensation of buildings obscured by falling snow.

The bus is shown again in *Fifth Avenue* (c. 1899; PLATE 7), a bustling street scene, which portrays the vehicle at an oblique angle as it moves through traffic. The placement of the bus and the vertical format may have been modeled on Alfred Stieglitz's famous 1893 photograph of a horse drawn stage in inclement weather, *Winter on Fifth Avenue*. Shinn would likely have known the photo as it was widely exhibited and subsequently published in 1897 in a volume of Stieglitz's New York scenes titled *Picturesque Bits of New York*.[81]

In 1900, *Fifth Avenue* and *Fifth Avenue Stage Coach*, (which is likely the original title of *Fifth Avenue Coach, Winter*) were exhibited in Shinn's first one-man show at Boussod, Valadon & Co., which later traveled to the Pennsylvania Academy.[82] The pictures elicited the praise of a reviewer who commented on the stages' anachronistic character noting, "New York's Fifth avenue, for example, never has been so sympathetically interpreted pictorially as in certain of Mr. Shinn's drawings. It is the Fifth avenue known to us all, with the busy crowds of scurrying people, the pompous policeman and the rickety old coaches, relics of an earlier civilization…."[83] Another writer commented, "In such a sketch as his "Fifth Avenue Stage Coach"…with one of its horses half-prostrate on the snowy pavement, Mr. Shinn has caught the spirit and the atmosphere of the time and place and incident…."[84] The old coach in a snowstorm remained a favored motif of Shinn. In 1914 he returned to the theme in his pastel, *Fifth Avenue Bus, 23rd Street and Broadway* (The National Gallery of Art, Washington, D.C.).

Lower Manhattan

In this phase as champion of the oppressed, he dreamed of forming a lever, alloyed and strengthened with his sympathy for the under dog that would some day rest on the flinty fulcrum of the backs of the rich and swerve the whole social muck and barren places around to the sunny fields of the deserving plenty.

— Everett Shinn, Shinn Autobiographical Material, Helen Farr Sloan Library, Delaware Art Museum, Wilmington

The pictures by the Ashcan artists of ethnic groups and the Lower East Side have drawn a variety of responses from scholars. Some have perceived the Ashcan artists' treatment of their subjects as euphemizing or distancing; always keeping the immigrant as a marked "other," separate from middle-class life.[85] Rebecca Zurier has addressed the question of how "real" was the depiction of New York immigrant life in the works of the Ashcan school. She notes that stereotypes did exist in the work of the Ashcan School, but no more so than in popular music and contemporary theater. [86] She continues by pointing out that even the so-called objective photography of the social reformer Jacob Riis has been shown in recent scholarship to sensationalize the lives of the urban poor.[87] Moreover, Riis's photographs were not "objective." Riis hoped to improve the living conditions of his subjects and therefore created photographs, which showed them under the worst possible conditions as a means of stimulating public sympathy and urban reform. Zurier also examines the more neutral photographs of the Byron Company, which produced stock photography to be sold to magazine editors and private clients. She points out that the Byron Company images actually present a more chaotic and confusing image of the Lower East Side than those that appeared in the work of the Ashcan artists. Zurier concludes, "This brief survey might tempt one to conclude that there was no objective representation of the Lower East Side, or perhaps no 'real' Lower East Side at all. We would argue instead that there were many true versions of the place. Each of these representations reveals aspects of historical reality — the neighborhood's appearance as well as the artists' experience of it."[88]

What was Shinn's experience of the Lower East Side? Unlike artists such as Abastenia St. Leger Eberle, Shinn never lived in the immigrant neighborhoods amongst the ethic communities he depicted. At the time that he was portraying the Lower East Side he was residing at 145 East 21st Street, a comfortable distance from the tenement area. As he became more critically and commercially successful, he moved to a brownstone off Washington Square and began summering at his second home in Plainfield, New Hampshire. In many ways Shinn's goals were more aligned with upper-class society and this

was the social group he sought to emulate. In 1911, when asked about his perception of himself, Shinn replied, "Personally I conform to decent, accepted standards of living and conduct, and a Bohemian is the last thing I consider myself, or should want any one else to consider me."[89] And yet despite his own physical, social, and economic distance from the inhabitants of the Lower East Side, Shinn managed to create some of the Ashcan School's most sympathetic renderings of the area.

During the second half of the 19th century, New York City experienced an enormous influx of immigrants. Arriving from countries such as Germany, Italy, Poland, Ireland, the Ukraine and China, they established their own ethnic enclaves. Luc Sante, who has written authoritatively on this topic, notes that after the revolution of 1848, Germans became the dominant population of the Lower East Side above Houston Street. Nearby were the Hungarians who occupied the areas east and south of the German neighborhood. The Jewish area radiated outward from the intersection of Canal, Essex and East Broadway. The Irish inhabited the region between Cherry Hill and Corlears Hook. Chinatown began in the 1870s on Mott and Pell Streets and radiated in four directions. Little Italy lay to the north of Chinatown.[90] Neighborhood boundaries, however, were not distinctly fixed and did not necessarily keep people separate. Rather, neighborhoods were in a con-

[FIG. 2] *Cross Streets of New York*, 1899
Charcoal, watercolor, white chalk, and
Chinese white on paper, 21⅝ x 29 inches
Corcoran Gallery of Art, Washington, D.C.

stant state of flux. As soon as one group
attained a level of prosperity it would
move to a wealthier quarter. In turn, the
vacated neighborhood would become
home to a new wave of immigrants, who
were likely to be poorer. In the overcrowded tenements, residents found
themselves encountering others whose
customs and way of life were unlike their
own. It was such "crossroads" where people from very divergent backgrounds
bumped up against each other that fascinated Shinn and became the subject of
his most original work.

Cross Streets of New York (1899; FIG. 2)
and *Park Row, Fruit Venders* (c. 1899;

PLATE 9) are exceptional examples Shinn's
depictions of urban interaction and life
on the streets of lower Manhattan. For
Shinn the crowded downtown streets
counterbalanced his pictures of uptown
locales and were essential for a complete
vision of contemporary New York. In his
unpublished autobiography he remarked:

> You have asked me why I like to
> paint streets, and particularly clut-
> tered ones…why, snow packed and
> slushed, and why the scattered and
> littered dams in gutters. Why the
> lamp posts and hydrants base that
> catch the drifts of wind blown lit-
> ter. If all I wished to paint should
> lie in…park walks, alley ways, ashe
> [sic] cans and garbage pails I would
> pass it bye [sic] holding my nose
> and kick the scattering disfigure-
> ment as I go for all of that is only
> half of it…. Just half of the meas-
> ure of all humanity. Just half of a
> picture of any city street.[91]

In *Cross Streets of New York,* the snow-
covered street is rutted with tracks from
wagons and pushcarts. On the left and
right sides of the street are dilapidated
buildings with unsteady looking fire
escapes and shutters coming loose from
their hinges. Clothing is displayed on
outside racks indicating that the area is
commercial as well as residential. In the
center foreground, an ash barrel is
prominently displayed. Behind the barrel
a man and woman are engaged in either
a dispute or a very animated discussion.

On the left, a man struggles to negotiate a pushcart through the snowy street. Like the ash barrel, the pushcart was an indicator that one had entered a less desirable section of the city. During the last quarter of the 19th century, the pushcart became a prominent feature of urban commerce. Selling everything from fruit to old shoes, pushcarts were extremely popular in immigrant neighborhoods where the population was familiar with the European street markets. Although pushcarts had previously existed in other areas of the city, their association with immigrants caused them to be shunned by residents of wealthier neighborhoods. As historian Daniel Bluestone states, "Once middle- and upper-class urban residents identified pushcarts as central to immigrant and working-class life, they often viewed the arrival of a pushcart market in a neighborhood as tangible evidence of undesirable demographic and social change."[92]

Pushcarts feature prominently in *Park Row, Fruit Venders* (c. 1899; PLATE 9), one of Shinn's most fascinating images of lower Manhattan.[93] According to Metropolitan historian Christopher Gray, the site is probably City Hall Park looking north along the east side of Park Row. In the background to the right is the iron streetcar terminal that leads off to the Brooklyn Bridge while the large building in the center with the triangular pediment is the Old Hall of Records, which was the oldest civic building in New York until demolished c. 1905.[94]

In the foreground at the right, a male figure with his back turned to the viewer strides into the congestion. He acts as the viewer's surrogate leading into the picture. A lady wearing a long blue coat and carrying an umbrella walks in front of him. The couple appears better dressed than the other figures suggesting that they are not residents of the neighborhood, but simply passing through perhaps on their way to the streetcar terminal in the background.

In the center of the picture, fruit is displayed on rickety pushcarts.[95] The bright yellow bananas and other fruit (possibly oranges) immediately attract the viewer's attention as well as that of the figures in the pastel. At the center right a well-dressed man gleefully reaches for his wallet to make a purchase from the cart. Bananas and oranges were expensive items and the delighted consumer is contrasted with less fortunate trio of a father with his two small children on the left who cannot afford such luxuries.[96] Although Shinn claimed that his pictures were not meant to induce urban reform, the pastel nevertheless generates sympathy for the city's poor.

In addition to contrasting rich and poor, *Park Row, Fruit Vendors* is notable for the inclusion of children, a relatively rare subject in Shinn's oeuvre. Unlike Bellows, Glackens, Sloan, Luks and Henri, who included children in some of their most well-known works, Shinn expressed little interest in Ashcan kids.[97] In an unusual departure for Shinn, he not only includes children in the work but also, through the use of red and pink pastel, draws the viewer's attention to them. Significantly, the children do not conform to the stereotype of the slum-child, which Doezema describes as: "Their figures are squat; their broad heads are adored with tattered hats or a thin crop of scraggly hair; they stand either slightly hunched over, or…with stomachs protruding; and they appear dull-witted and slow-moving."[98] Nor are they like the rowdy kids in *Street Fight* (1907; Dr. and Mrs. Robert Nowinski Collection) by George Bellows or the disheveled, mischievous children who appear in his work, *On the East Side* (c. 1907; Mead Art Museum). Rather, the boy and girl in *Park Row, Fruit Vendors* stand quietly at their father's side. They are humbly, but neatly dressed and peer curiously out at the viewer. Their good behavior contrasts both with contemporary interpretations of slum children, and quite humorously, with another of Shinn's representations of children, those featured in *Madison Square and the Dewey Arch* (1899; Location Unknown). In the latter pastel, a well dressed, clearly upper-class little girl is seen struggling and protesting as her mother attempts to walk with her through the park. Although Shinn may not have intended the pastels to be read as such, they can be interpreted as subverting stereotypical notions that social class defined good or bad behavior.

Of the variety of Lower East Side subjects that Shinn chose to portray, the ragpicker is the theme to which he returned most often.[99] According to Sante, ragpicking was considered the lowest level of commerce.[100] Ragpickers combed through ash barrels or solicited door to door for items that had been discarded. A typical ragman's abode is described as housing "bones, broken dishes, rags, bits of furniture, cinders, old tin, useless lamps, decaying vegetables, ribbons, cloths, legless chairs, and carrion, all mixed together and heaped up nearly to the ceiling, leaving barely enough room for a bed on the floor."[101] These items were generally repaired if possible and sold on the streets from pushcarts, or occasionally from stores. Perhaps it was the extreme pathos of the ragpicker — his lonely plight and dire circumstances — that attracted Shinn. He may also have been influenced by Raffaëlli (although Shinn later claimed to dislike Raffaëlli's work) whose exhibition at Durand-Ruel Galleries in New York in 1899 included two pictures of ragpickers.

Shinn first exhibited a pastel of a ragpicker in 1900 at Boussod, Valadon & Co. Titled *Rag Picker*, this may have been the same pastel that was reproduced in May 1900 in *The Bookman* as *The Ragpicker*.[102] In the illustration, a man is stooped over an ash barrel sifting through the waste. Behind him, the snow-covered ground is littered with broken shutters, indicating that the location is a poor tenement neighborhood. Shinn's pictures of ragpickers received considerable attention by reviewers who admired the subject's gutsy treatment and originality. In February 1901 when Shinn exhibited *The Rag Picker* at J. Eastman Chase's Gallery in Boston, reviewers marveled at the artist's ability to portray a squalid urban subject in a manner that was not only not offensive but which also exhibited "charm" and "quaintness." Upon seeing *The Rag Picker* one writer responded:

> The Rag Picker is a curious, gloomy little composition full of a strange charm, none the less. One would hate to be there; but, my dear sir, what has that got to do with it? The picture is delightful in the quaintness of the crazy, broken shutters and the hideous hodge podge of staved-in barrels.

> And amid the abomination of desolations stands an old prophet of a chiffonier and poker among the "debris." The thing is full of character and energy — the darks are, perhaps, a trifle blackish — the fierceness of the handling, perhaps, creates a rather scratchy effect; but none the less it makes a very distinct impression on one.[103]

Another reviewer compared Shinn's "ugly" themes to the work of great writers noting:

> It has been Mr. Shinn's usual preference to deal with what might be called the seamy side of its [New York's] scenery. One remembers a typical picture among his score of pastels which is something like this: A rag-picker at work in the tenement-house district, bending over a decrepit barrel, one of a heap of half-broken and ruined barrels piled up just outside a forlorn brick building, which might be regarded as a study in battered shutters; a place of peculiar and hopeless ugliness and poverty, of pathetic neglectedness and filthiness. Out of such materials Mr. Shinn constructs a picture of distinct interest, working as sympathetically over its details as Balzac or Dickens worked over the details of their descriptive passages about some greasy, musty, hideous corners of Paris and London.[104]

Shinn's interest in down-and-out types was not limited to New York. Interspersed with his more glamorous pictures of Paris and London are accounts such as *Green Park, London* (1908; PLATE 10) and *Street Corner in Paris* (1905; PLATE 11). In the latter work, Shinn returns to the ragpicker motif, however, the indigent man is no longer the central attraction and the neighborhood is no longer run-down. Rather, the setting of this watercolor is a well-tended street corner with immaculate sidewalks and carefully preserved buildings. The subject of the picture emphasizes the quotidian activities of Parisian life. As the figure at the far left sifts through an ash barrel, the man at the right, who is probably opening his shop for the day, removes a protective board from the window. Indeed, *Street Corner, Paris* may be the same watercolor Shinn showed in 1935 in an exhibition at the Morton Galleries, New York as *Opening Shop…Paris*.[105] The work, in which areas of wash effectively convey the impression of melting snow, reveals Shinn's skill at handling the watercolor medium.

Relationships and Recognition: "A man who only has to go forward…"

Both from a personal and professional standpoint 1899 proved to be an extremely important year for Shinn. It was the year that he first began to show his work professionally and the beginning of important connections with people such as Elsie de Wolfe, Stanford White, Clyde Fitch, and Julia Marlowe. De Wolfe is remembered today as a legend in American interior design, responsible for sweeping away Victorian clutter and replacing heavy curtains and red velvet with English chintz and French toiles.[106] Shinn met de Wolfe shortly after she had triumphantly restyled the Irving Place house she shared with her companion Elisabeth "Bessie" Marbury. Though her reputation as a decorator was growing, at the time Shinn met de Wolfe she was

focused on her career as an actress. Throughout the 1890s de Wolfe appeared in a succession of roles under Charles Frohman's management at the Empire Theater and it is possible that Shinn met the actress at one of these performances.[107]

At the same time that Shinn befriended Marlowe and De Wolfe, he also received his first invitation to show his work in a museum exhibition. In January of 1899 five of Shinn's pastels were shown at the Pennsylvania Academy's annual exhibition. According to Shinn's record book he showed *Elevated Station*, *Fifth Avenue*, *The Docks*, *Housetops-Rainy Day*, and *Street Scene*. The pastels received considerable praise in the press. On January 15, 1899 the Philadelphia *Press* noted:

> There is a row of black and white studies of New York streets by Mr. Everett Shinn in the corridor which reveal a new artist on the walls, a man who only has to go forward to fill the full measure of success in the work of making the life of the day and the pavement interpret and express the emotion and observation of all time.[108]

On January 27, 1899 the *Monitor Register* of Woodstown announced that the Academy exhibition included "Several excellent drawings in watercolors by Mr. Everett Shinn."[109] Shinn's youth combined with the fact that he had just recently been a student at the Academy, made his accomplishment all the more impressive.

Shinn sold his first picture, a pastel titled *Street Scene*, from the exhibition to the well-known artist William Merritt Chase. Shinn was so honored to have his picture admired by Chase that when he learned of Chase's interest in the pastel, he offered to give it to him. Shinn recalled Chase's response to the potential gift, "Lifting his quizical [sic] one eyebrow when I wanted to give it to him he said 'No…young man…we can all give pictures away…there is always someone that will accept them…but to give up money for our pictures is a gesture from a public we must not ignore…thank you just the same…I now own a Shinn and it cost me money.'"[110]

Shinn's subsequent attempts to exhibit work met with a mixed response. His nine submissions to the Society of American Artists were all rejected as were the four pastels sent to the National Academy of Design. He did succeed in exhibiting several works at the Association of Allied Arts at the Berkeley Lyceum from April 10 to 15, 1899; one work at the Kit-Kat Club from April 8 to 15, 1899, which was purchased from the exhibition; and two pastels at the St. Louis Exposition from September 11 to October 14, 1899.[111] His big break however resulted from his friendship with Elsie de Wolfe.

Elsie De Wolfe was socially well connected and her home served as a meeting place for performers, artists, and writers. From November 7 to 17, 1899, De Wolfe's salon became a temporary art gallery hosting a small exhibition of five pastels by Shinn. Not only did the show provide exposure for Shinn's work, but it also resulted in two sales. *Wharf Fight* was purchased by a private collector and *Scene — Julia Marlowe* was sold to the playwright Clyde Fitch. Through De Wolfe, Shinn made the acquaintance of the architect Stanford White. White was impressed with Shinn's work and questioned him about his pastels:

> WHITE: These are splendid.
> What are you going to do with them?
> SHINN: Sell them if possible.
> WHITE: Ever try to have an exhibition?
> SHINN : Yes, Last week at Boussod and Valadon, but Mr. Glenzer said my work doesn't interest him.
> WHITE : Is that what Mr. Glezer said? When do you want to open your exhibition?
> SHINN : Where?
> WHITE: There.
> How many pictures do you have?
> SHINN: About forty.
> WHITE: Go up and see Glenzer. Name your date and you will open.[112]

White arranged for Boussod, Valadon & Co. to offer Shinn his first major one-man exhibition. The show, composed of forty-four pastels, was to be on view from February 26 until March 10, 1900.[113] The pastels were shown against red walls and, though the frames were thought crude, the work itself was deemed by one reviewer "fit to hang on the Milky Way."[114] Overall the exhibition was judged an immense critical and commercial success. Stanford White and Elsie de Wolfe marshaled their considerable influence and encouraged friends and patrons to purchase works. Of the 44 pastels exhibited, 30 were sold.[115] For the next six years, until his death in 1906, White would continue to be a great supporter of Shinn's work.[116]

Critics immediately noted Shinn's sudden rise to fame. One reviewer expressing her surprise at Shinn's startling debut on the New York art scene commented:

> Everett Shinn may have had the usual difficulties and preparation that seem to be part of the schooling of the artist, but in New York, at least, he had simply "arrived" before he had been heard of to any extent. His recent exhibition at the gallery Boussod, Valadon and Company, where he exposed a number of pastels representing mainly street scenes of the metropolis, was one of the most attractive exhibits of the season, and as an individual showing, it stood comparison with like exhibits of several years past.[117]

Although his draftsmanship was considered shaky by some commentators, in general he was deemed full of promise. One reviewer proclaimed that the exhi-

bition was "far from commonplace… revealing a little known worker who must now, unless all signs fail, emerge from obscurity."[118] In addition, writers commented on his personal style, which was called "spirited" and "quite refreshing." However, more than any other aspect of his work, critics discussed Shinn's choice of subject matter, which promptly identified him as a chronicler of the New York city streets. One critic remarked, "There was not, however, anything in that early work to foretell the keen appreciation and insight into the very essence of city life which have made Mr. Shinn's New York street scenes so immediately appreciated."[119] As another writer poetically phrased it:

> The work returns to us like music. The life is caught up and runs out in strokes like memory that dreams. Madison Square is there in all its night beauty, with the white arch shining like a woman's flesh and shouldering out the gloom; red housetops; in snow, and cleared by rain, lean hard against each other; Broadway and Twenty-third Street is vivisected down to the very core, and the art evades us; the docks, a foundry, the music halls, Park Row, Union Square, are put on paper with a few lines of pastel in a way that wipes out all of this kind that has gone before. The whole history of the Fifth Avenue Stage Line is written clear. What the Cooper Union Fountain does

is told. The ragpicker rises like a wraith and records his benumbing days. Hester Street look sullenly towards Fifth Avenue. A downtown shop gives out the whole history of the neighborhood.[120]

Moreover, the reviewer recognized Shinn's pastels as a means for helping people to make sense of the city. At the exhibition, people could glimpse the diversity of Manhattan. Images of ragpickers from the Lower East Side, dock workers from the waterfront, and well-dressed ladies from Madison Square were all brought together and placed side by side on the gallery walls. Although viewers may have been able to identify with only a few of the people in the pastels, as a whole they would have recognized the disparate elements as forming a picture of greater New York. The critic noted, "Street-scene after street scene takes you into lives the existence of which you had guessed faintly; and through it all the time of day, the million mutations of beauty we call weather, the lime-light, gaslight, sunlight, slush, cold, drip, wind, sleet, and life of this great city flashes and recedes and comes again."[121]

Shinn's treatment of pastel also elicited comment. His technique of rapidly applied pastel strokes aptly translated the bustle and movement of the city. At close inspection, his figures are often hastily sketched outlines with spots of color, but viewed from a distance they emerge as convincingly readable forms.

While the works' lack of finish was startling and offensive to some writers, one perceptive critic praised Shinn for finding a new vocabulary with which to interpret the speed of modern life. He noted, "There are those who often complain that the modern advanced spirits of the time have ideas, but not the technique to interpret them. This cannot be said of Everett Shinn."[122] Not only does his technique effectively capture the congestion of a busy street corner, but it also, on a larger scale, records an era of New York history that was rapidly fading. It is as if in his quick sketchy lines, Shinn wanted to arrest a moment of history before it disappeared entirely. When compared to the revolutionary treatment of movement in the work of the Futurists and Cubists, Shinn's aesthetic does not look very progressive. However, in 1900, the work's spontaneity and freedom of execution were seen as an affront to prescribed canons of finish and an effort to depict the "modern."

Inevitably Shinn's work was compared with that of other artists. His depictions of the city in inclement weather drew laudatory remarks, one critic noting "Even Childe Hassam has not given as good an idea and impression of the streets as of New York in Winter as does Mr. Shinn in the present display."[123] Others saw the European influences of Honoré Daumier,[124] but more often Shinn was called the "American Raffaëlli." The association was underscored by an article that claimed

Raffaëlli had come to see Shinn's Boussod, Valadon & Co. exhibition and acknowledged his influence on the younger artist remarking, " Very, very good. He is a *leetle* bit my son."[125] Years later Shinn rebuffed any influence of Raffaëlli, stating "I resented the implication of parentage as I had always heartily disliked his work."[126]

The exhibition at Boussod, Valadon & Co. was scheduled to close on March 10, 1900 after which it was to travel to Philadelphia and Cincinnati. However, due to the show's popularity with the public and the positive critical response, the exhibition was extended to April 4. On April 9, a reconfigured version of the show opened at the Pennsylvania Academy. The number of works was increased to sixty-five and included a group of fourteen small pastel sketches, which were in the show, but not listed in the catalogue. Just the previous year, when Shinn exhibited five works at the Pennsylvania Academy, the pastels were hung ignominiously in the corridor. Following his success in New York, Shinn's pictures were given a considerably better position in one of the Academy's small galleries. As in New York they caught the attention of several critics who noted the artist's skill at portraying the urban environment.

Boussod, Valadon & Co., realizing that they had "discovered" a promising young artist, offered to send Everett and Flossie to Europe. During their sojourn the Shinns would visit Paris and London where Everett was expected to develop ideas for an exhibition to be held be at Boussod, Valadon & Co. in 1901. The gallery would cover expenses and in return their firm would handle all resultant work. Shortly after the close of Shinn's show at the Pennsylvania Academy, Everett and Flossie spent a week in Woodstown with his family. In the middle of May they sailed for Europe and Shinn embarked on a new phase of his career.[127]

London and Paris

The Shinns' stay in Europe lasted about six months from May 19 through October 6, 1900.[128] Unlike so many American artists who went to Europe at the end of the 19th century, Shinn did not study at the Académie Julian or the Ecole des Beaux Arts and attempted no private instruction while abroad. Unfortunately, there is very little written documentation of the trip. If Shinn wrote any letters to friends at home, they are not located. His unpublished autobiography provides some information, but many details remain unknown. The best records of what Shinn saw during his sojourn are the dozens of sketches of Paris and London. Some of these small drawings, most measuring 5 x 7 inches, are complete works of art in themselves; others provided the preliminary material for finished pictures.

London was the Shinns' first port of call where Everett worked briefly before heading to Paris, a city in which he was much more inspired. In his 1901 exhibition at Boussod, Valadon & Co., where Shinn exhibited the results of his trip to Europe, he showed only six pictures that can be identified as English subjects, compared with more than forty French subjects.[129] His attention to London's major intersections and squares is evidenced in two of his sketches, which depict Trafalgar Square. While in London, Shinn also took time to wander through the museums carefully studying the pictures and, in at least one instance, copying a painting. Shinn's *Robert Le Diable*, 1901, is a copy of *The Ballet Scene from Meyerbeer's Opera "Robert le Diable,"* painted by Edgar Degas in 1876. The picture had just been given to the Victoria and Albert Museum in 1900, making it the first painting by Degas to enter the collection of an English museum.[130] News reports of the important gift may have drawn Shinn's attention to the painting, which in subject matter would have struck a note with his passion for the theater. In Degas, Shinn found an artist who not only shared his concerns for performers on stage, but did so it a way that was radically unconventional. Degas's cropped composition, use of oblique angles, and attention to the audience underscored the picture's sense of immediacy making it seem daringly modern. Shinn would subsequently adopt these devices in his own work earning him another title: the "American Degas."

About mid-June,[131] the Shinns left London for Paris where Everett found a studio in the Latin Quarter on the Rue Notre Dame des Champs.[132] The Montparnasse area had long been a favorite site for artists and on the Rue Notre Dame des Champs one could find more studios than on any other Parisian street. Artists who once had studios on the street included Carolus-Duran at No. 58, Rosa Bonheur at No. 61, and Adolphe-William Bouguereau at No. 75.[133] The low cost of studio space and the camaraderie of neighboring artists probably helped attract Shinn to the district.

From his studio window Shinn claimed to have seen Edgar Degas, "when the tall old gentleman would venture out of his house across from my studio."[134] Having just studied and copied *Robert Le Diable* in London, Shinn must have been thrilled to see the artist himself. He referred to Degas as "the greatest painter France has ever turned out" and may have been inspired by the Frenchman's mastery of the figure to improve his own articulation of the human form.[135] Models were easily hired at a model's market that took place every Monday at the corner of the Rue de la Grande Chaumière and the Boulevard Montparnasse, very close to the Rue Notre Dame de Champs. Perhaps in an effort to improve his draftsmanship and to emulate the French master, Shinn hired the same woman who had posed for Degas; he later told a group of art students that the woman who posed as the elegant lady in an opera box was Degas's model.[136] In addition to professional models, Shinn invited dancers to his studio, but instead of posing them in a conventional fashion, he asked them to perform. As they leapt and twirled, Shinn made many small sketches that he later used to develop larger paintings.[137]

James McNeill Whistler was also a familiar figure in the area and it is possible that Shinn moved there to be close to Whistler's studio. In 1888, Whistler had settled into a house on the Rue du Bac, and between the years 1892 and 1901 he maintained a studio on the Rue Notre Dame des Champs at No. 86.[138] Whistler by then was immensely well known and respected in France. In 1891 the Louvre had purchased his famous painting *Arrangement in Grey and Black: Portrait of the Painter's Mother*, making it the first painting by an American artist to enter the museum. Americans flocked to his studio to buy things, have their portraits painted, or to study with him. Nearby was the Académie Carmen opened by the model Carmen Rossi, where Whistler taught intermittently and which became a magnet for an international group of students. Although there is no evidence that Shinn ever met Whistler, the artist's teachings were very much a part of the artistic climate of the time and therefore would have been known to Shinn.

Shinn would also have had ample opportunity to view the work of Whistler at the Exposition Universelle et Internationale de Paris. Everett and Flossie arrived in the middle of the Exposition (open from April 15 to November 12, 1900), and spent time wandering through the exhibits while Shinn recorded vignettes for future pictures.[139] In the U. S. galleries of the Grand Palais, Whistler and John Singer Sargent were celebrated as the figures most representative of the artistic identity of the United States. Whistler was represented by three works: *Brown and Gold*, c. 1895–1900; *Mother of Pearl and Silver: The Andalusian*, c. 1894; and *The Little White Girl: Symphony in White, No. 11*, 1864.[140] Not far away, at the Musée du Luxembourg, Shinn would have been able to see Whistler's most well-known painting, *Arrangement in Grey and Black: Portrait of the Painter's Mother*, 1871, which had been particularly admired by Robert Henri:

> About the portrait Whistler painted of his mother I have always had a great feeling of beauty. She is old. But there is something in her face and gesture that tells of the integrity of her life…. There she sits, and in her poise one reads the history of a splendid personality. She is at once so gentle, so experienced, and so womanly strong.[141]

The numerous sketches that Shinn made on his trip to Europe in 1900 provided the raw material for more that a decade of work depicting the French capital. The pastels and paintings of Paris he produced over the next several years reveal hours spent wandering the streets carefully observing the local environment. Prior to Shinn's visit, the city had recently undergone a building program that made it one of the most modern and well laid out urban spaces in the world. Parks had been built and new avenues constructed creating a pleasant atmosphere for strolling and people watching. Experiences in the Luxembourg Gardens were recorded in his notebooks for future pictures and his visits to French music halls and café-concerts became the material for later pastels such as *Outdoor Stage, Paris* (undated; PLATE 54).

Though Shinn's output in Paris consisted primarily of sketches, he did complete some finished works. On July 3 Goupil's in Paris, an affiliation of Boussod, Valadon & Co. in New York, showed four new pastels by Shinn: *The Wrestlers, Merry-Go-Round, Monkey Cart* and *Luxembourg Garden — Punch & Judy Show*.[142]

Shinn's friend Elsie de Wolfe and her companion Elisabeth Marbury were also in France and Everett and Flossie took the opportunity to visit them at their summer home. In 1899, De Wolfe and Marbury had taken a three-year lease on an elegant pavilion at Versailles, where during the summers they entertained a small, cultivated circle that included Henry Adams and the American painter Walter Gay.[143] When the Shinns arrived they found themselves in the company of Mr. Joseph Hunt, M. Jean Richepin

(the French playwright), his wife Mme. Jean Richepin, Miss Marie Tempest, Mr. David Belasco, and Mr. Cosmo Lennox.[144] The occasion provided Shinn's first introduction to Belasco, the American playwright, who six years later would commission a large mural project from Shinn for his New York theater, The Stuyvesant.

The Shinns departed for New York on October 6, 1900 sailing from Cherbourg on the S. S. Minnehaha. Returning to New York on October 15, they re-settled at 122 East 19th Street. Shinn had exactly three months to prepare for his second exhibition at Boussod, Valadon & Co., which opened January 15 and was on view through February 23, 1901. Titled "Paris Types" (the name was likely a reference to an exhibition by Raffaëlli called "Les Types de Paris") it consisted of 46 pastels, plus 33 uncatalogued works, and six additional works, which he listed as "extra ballet girls." The grouping was predominantly Parisian subjects, but also included several scenes of London and four views of New York.

The exhibition was reviewed in many papers, but the critics were strangely divided about the show's merits. Some felt that Shinn's draughtsmanship had improved and commended his ability to record the salient aspects of everyday Parisian life.[145] A reviewer who distinguished Shinn's unconventional use of pastel from the more traditional treatment of the medium opined, "They are not like the pastels known to a former generation of picture lovers, those smooth views of river trees and distant mountains, with soft edges and pasty reflections, and no character anywhere. Perhaps the works of Mr. Shinn go a little too far in the opposite direction in the way of dash, sparkle and contrast."[146] Others felt that the exhibition was technically weaker than that of the previous year, complaining that the artist whom they had deemed full of promise, had disappointed them with sloppy execution.[147] Compositions were judged facile and ideas partially realized. Moreover, one critic felt that the European works did not look distinctly different from those depicting American subject matter, noting a "family resemblance" amongst the works depicting New York and those of Paris and London.[148] However, despite some negative criticism, the show was commercially successful. Shinn sold several pastels including five works to his Chicago patron Mrs. Chauncey Blair and two to Mrs. J. P. Morgan.

While his show at Boussod, Valadon & Co. was still on view he also held an exhibition at J. Eastman Chase's Gallery in Boston of 20 works, all New York scenes. From November 6 to 31, 1901, Shinn held his second major exhibition that year at Boussod, Valadon & Co. This time the subjects were primarily American. The perhaps chauvinistic critics were delighted by his return to Gotham themes. One remarked, "[he] once more and wisely, returns to New York and its neighborhood for his subjects."[149]

Shinn had clearly "arrived." With three successful New York exhibitions and European travel under his belt, he was ready to enter the established art community. In the fall of 1901 he became one of the chief instructors at the New York School of Art, teaching a class on illustration, which met for an hour every afternoon.[150] Although the position was ultimately short lived (Henri took over the class in 1902), during his brief tenure there Shinn was an active member of the school. In addition to teaching, he participated in the school's Arts and Crafts Club and served on its exhibition committee.[151] He showed two works in the annual exhibition of the watercolor club at the Boston Art Club and also continued his magazine illustration.

Shinn's prosperity was growing, as was his social standing. In July 1901 the *Brooklyn Daily Eagle* reported that Shinn was spending a few days at Sea Cliff, a popular summer resort in Nassau County.[152] After his return from Europe, though he continued to paint gritty New York, he focused increasingly on the glamour of uptown life. Indeed, as Shinn stated in a 1952 interview, "Actually because I wasn't as interested as the others in people sleeping under bridges…I was often accused then of being a social snob. Not at all — it's just that the uptown life with all its glitter was more good-looking. The people made pictures."[153] With the sale of several works and good prospects for future exhibitions, Shinn was feeling comfortable enough financially to invest in a home in Plainfield, New Hampshire where, from 1902–1907, the Shinns summered and took part in the in the Cornish Colony. Although outside the scope of this essay, the time that Shinn spent in Cornish is a fascinating and little documented period of his career.

Figure and Fantasy

The six months spent in Europe were to have a significant effect on Shinn's oeuvre. Although ultimately he would remain committed to modern life subject matter, the experience in Paris not only broadened his artistic horizons but also encouraged him to pursue new subject matter and new media. Following his trip, the human figure begins to play a more prominent role in his art. Dancers and theater imagery start to compete with city scenes, eventually becoming the subjects with which Shinn is most often associated. In 1901, he exhibited his first oil, a theater subject titled *The Ballet Dancer*, c. 1901.[154] Although he would not have a major exhibition of oils until 1905, the introduction of oil paint and the focus on the dancer are indicative of the future direction of Shinn's oeuvre and will be explored in the latter part of this essay.

In a departure from his typical engagement with the public space, beginning around 1902 Shinn began to represent the figure in the intimate domestic

sphere. Pastels of women bathing, created in 1903, strongly suggest the influence of Degas. *Girl in Bathtub* (1903; PLATE 12) recalls the pastels of female bathers that obsessed Degas during the final decades of his career.[155] In an article in the *International Studio* A. E. Gallatin commented on the influence of Degas on Shinn:

> Everett Shinn…has been greatly influenced by the art of Degas. But Shinn has only gone to Degas for inspiration, for ideas, not slavishly to copy him…. And Shinn has learnt another thing from Degas; he has learnt to draw. Look over his many portfolios of studies and sketches made from the nude…and you will see drawings powerful in their draughtsmanship, studies entirely free from all taint of the academic, drawings that proclaim him to be an artist possessing really great gifts.[156]

Girl in the Bathtub reveals Shinn's increasing skill in rendering anatomy. Not only is the figure confidently drawn, but Shinn also manages to make her appear poised despite the somewhat awkward position of getting in (or out) of the bathtub. The elegant, restrained palette so typical of Shinn's early pastels is again evident here.

In addition to the work of Degas another artistic lineage inspired Shinn — that of the French 18th century. Elsie de Wolfe, an ardent admirer of French painting and antiques, most likely introduced Shinn to the work of artists such as Jean-Antoine Watteau, Jean-Honoré Fragonard, and François Boucher. *Boudoir Scene* (1907; PLATE 13), *Young Woman in Her Boudoir* (1912; PLATE 14), and *At the Fountain* (c. 1925; PLATE 15) reveal the influence of the French 18th century, particularly the work of Fragonard.[157] The impact of the French Rococo is first reflected in dozens of red chalk drawings depicting women at their toilet or dressing created shortly after Shinn's return from Europe. By 1903 he had produced enough work in red chalk to send a book of drawings to M. Knoedler & Co.[158] and to lend a selection of work including one red chalk drawing and a book of nudes (presumably these were also red chalk drawings) to Stanford White.[159] Shinn continued to exhibit his red chalk drawings of nudes at New York galleries where they were well received. Henri Pène du Bois called him the "Fragonard of the Present Time" remarking, "None ever used it [red chalk] so aptly than Everett Shinn in figures of women, nude or draped, at the bath or in the dressing-room, in sketches of familiar scenes indoors or out of doors."[160] Beginning around 1907, Shinn created a small group of boudoir scenes. Among this selection *Boudoir Scene* and *Young Women in Her Boudoir* are unusual as they are executed in pastel rather than red chalk. Although the two pastels of boudoir scenes were completed five years apart, they are remarkably similar. Both

portray a woman in a state of dishabille within an 18th century interior. Though the scenes are ostensibly domestic, both include elements of theatricality. The blue draperies are drawn back like theater curtains revealing a model who strikes a pose as if she were aware that she is being watched. The boudoir pastel thus becomes a kind of keyhole spectacle.

At the Fountain (c. 1925; PLATE 15) with its array of powdered and wigged Rococo figures enjoying the pleasures of music in a park or garden is related stylistically to Shinn's decorative commissions. Beginning in 1905 with two ceilings, double doors, and a decorated piano completed in the manner of the French Rococo for the playwright Clyde Fitch, Shinn embarked on a career as a decorator that paralleled his position as an interpreter of modern life. In an article in 1905 Shinn expressed his delight with the Rococo style:

> When you speak the words Louis XIV, you have visions of ribbons and laces, of garlands, of theatrical fêtes under spreading trees with tapestries stretched out from branch to branch, of beribboned walking sticks and powdered wigs, of frivolity in life and its counterpart in art. I believe I have caught that evanescent charm — at least I have made the effort.[161]

Such charm is clearly evident in *At the Fountain*, which captures the spirit of fantasy and frivolity of the French Rococo. Frolicking ladies and gentlemen are rendered in quick sure strokes of pink, yellow and blue pastel. The entire composition is united by an overall bluish tonality. The pastel is possibly a study for one of Shinn's mural decorations. Indeed, the figure on the right playing a musical instrument resembles a similarly placed harlequin or court jester who appears on an elaborately painted door (Location Unknown) that Shinn completed for the George H. Townsend House in 1925. No satisfactory answer explains the outline of the circle on the pastel, but it is possible that Shinn considered excerpting part of the design for a ceiling panel or an over-the-door lunette.

New York City Scenes After 1900

Mr. Shinn's New York street scenes and glimpses of the environs of the city are among the best things of the kind yet painted by an American artist.
— Chicago *Record-Herald*, June 9, 1901[162]

Prior to Shinn's trip to Europe, his depictions of New York City focused predominantly on views of the urban arena as seen by the casual passerby. Back in Manhattan, Shinn continued this strategy, but expanded his repertoire reflecting changes in his life and that of the city. He maintained his interest in the working class and the plight of the urban poor, but also began to focus attention on commercial and leisure activities such as shopping and theater going. Occasionally he depicted a panoramic view as in *The East River at Night* (1906; PLATE 16), but more often he gave precedence to human activities. He also started to concentrate on different areas of the city, for example, Washington Square and Central Park.

Squares and Parks

Shinn was one of the great interpreters of New York City's parks and squares. He depicted Union Square Park, Madison Square Park, Washington Square Park, Gramercy Park and Central Park in what were to become some of his most striking accounts of the city's crossroads. *Nocturne, Gramercy Park* (1901; PLATE 17), one of the first parks scenes Shinn completed after his return from Europe, is an exceptional example of his ability to evoke a dramatic nighttime scene. The high vantage point Shinn employs in *Nocturne, Gramercy Park* is rare in his work as he generally represented his subjects at street level, increasing the dynamism between the subject and the viewer. Here he adopts a bird's eye perspective like that of the French Impressionists (for example Camille Pissaro, whose work he would have recently seen in France). Shinn probably created the pastel from the upper story window of an apartment building on Gramercy Park. The view, hemmed in on both sides by the dark mass of a building on the left and the red brick structure on the right, looks out upon a nighttime political rally or parade. Indeed, Shinn's record books list a pastel titled *Street Parade, Gramercy Park*, which may be the original title of this work. The marching figures carry candles, which form a dazzling line of yellow lights while above them exploding fireworks or Roman candles illuminate the night.

Nocturne, Gramercy Park is closely related to a pastel titled *Election Banner, Madison Square* (1903; PLATE 18). The work features a large billowing banner upon which are displayed the portraits of political candidates. The banner, however, is overshadowed by the stunning display of fireworks exploding into luminous cascades of showering light. Shinn's use of strokes of bright almost iridescent pastel is extremely effective in evoking the shimmer of incandescent light as it illuminates the nocturnal scene. Dazzling reflections are created on the street below where pedestrians become mere silhouettes, anonymous observers of the dramatic scene.

Both *Nocturne, Gramercy Park* and *Election Banner, Madison Square* are part of a loose grouping of pastels that feature dramatic pyrotechnics and dazzling lighting effects. Completed between 1900-1905 these "nocturnes" are probably informed by the work of Whistler — specifically the painting *Nocturne in Black and Gold: The Falling Rocket* (1875; The Detroit Institute of Arts). Shinn had been aware of Whistler's work since his student days at the Pennsylvania Academy, but it may have taken the famous pastel *Nocturne in Black and Gold: The Falling Rocket* to catalyze his admiration for the artist. The picture was internationally known due to the lawsuit that resulted when John Ruskin, in reference to this picture, accused Whistler of "flinging a pot of paint in the public's face." Whistler sued Ruskin for libel and the resulting trial became a media event. *Nocturne in Black and Gold: The Falling Rocket* was exhibited from January 15 to February 24, 1900 at The Sixty-ninth Annual Exhibition of the Pennsylvania Academy of the Fine Arts where Shinn would have had the opportunity to see it. In addition to *Nocturne, Gramercy Park* and *Election Banner, Madison Square* other works that may be considered "nocturnes" include *Fire on Mott Street* (1902; PLATE 23), *Fire on Twenty-Fourth Street* (1907; Cheekwood Museum of Art), and *Bastille Day* (1905; The Detroit Institute of Arts). Although it is difficult to confirm, it seems probable that Shinn conceived these pictures for his book "New York by Night," which he continued to work on after his return from Europe. A reporter who visited Shinn in 1901 recalled seeing "the remarkable book 'New York by Night' lying about his studio on 19th street."[163]

Central Park

From the fall of 1900, Shinn turned his attention to Central Park and in 1901 he exhibited four Central Park pictures: *Children — Central Park*, *A Bypath, Central Park*, *Thaw — Central Park*, and *Bridle Path Central Park* at Boussod, Valadon & Co. Prior to his trip abroad, he depicted Central Park only once in a now unlocated pastel shown in his Pennsylvania Academy exhibition of 1900. It seems that during his first years in New York, Shinn had little interest in Central Park. Not only was the park relatively far away from where he lived, but also its segregated environment was anathema to the urban dynamism he was fond of depicting.[164] While Madison Square, situated at the crossroads of two of New York's major streets, was very much of the city, Central Park was insulated from the bustle of metropolitan life. By blocking out the city and avoiding central allées, Olmstead and Vaux sought to create a rural landscape park modeled after the rambling English garden rather than its more structured French counterpart. The result was that Central Park lacked a focal point. For Shinn, who preferred the city's crossroads where social and economic diversity were concentrated in a limited space, Central Park may have been difficult to get an aesthetic hold upon.

Shinn certainly would have known the pictures of Central Park by other artists, particularly those by William Merritt

[FIG. 3] *Untitled (Park Scene),* c. 1901
Pastel on paper, 8⅛ x 11⅝ inches (sight)
Gibbes Museum of Art, Charleston,
South Carolina

Chase, the first artist to become
identified with the Park.[165] When Chase
first painted Central Park in 1889, it was
in the process of becoming more democratic. During its first thirteen years, the
park had been enjoyed primarily by the
city's richest five percent. Working-class
people were present in the park, but due
to their six-day-a-week work schedule,
tended to use the park on different days
than the upper classes.[166] By the 1890s the
park's demographics were shifting toward
greater diversity, but Chase, in pictures
such as *Lake for Miniature Sailboats,
Central Park* (c. 1890; Peter G. Terian)
and *In the Park a By-Path* (1890–91;
Thyssen-Bornemisza Collection) still
portrayed it as a decorous landscape fre-

quented by women and well-behaved
children. Ten years later, when Shinn's
colleagues Ernest Lawson, Maurice
Prendergast and William Glackens portrayed the park, they represented a
broader spectrum of the city's social classes and racial groups. Glackens, in
particular in pictures such as *The Drive,
Central Park* (c. 1905; The Cleveland
Museum of Art), showed the mixture of
classes that enjoyed Central Park.

Though he was aware of the renditions of
the park by other artists, Shinn's interest
in Central Park was most likely inspired
by his experience and delight in the
Luxembourg Gardens of Paris where he
spent hours recording the genteel environment. In New York he utilized these
notations to complete larger pastels of
the Luxembourg Gardens and in 1901 he
showed *Merry-Go-Round (Luxembourg
Gardens), Punch and Judy Show
(Luxembourg Gardens), The Milliner's Girl
(Luxembourg Gardens), Sunset (Luxembourg
Gardens), Storm in Luxembourg Gardens,*
and *A Sudden Shower (Luxembourg
Gardens).* It is probably *A Sudden Shower
(Luxembourg Gardens)* to which a critic
refers in a review of Shinn's 1901 exhibition. He writes, "He carries us to the
gardens of the Luxembourg, where a
sudden squall is driving everyone to
shelter."[167] In 1902, Shinn created another version of the Luxembourg Gardens
during a shower in the work *Spring
Shower in Luxembourg Park, Paris* (1902;
PLATE 19). The lushly colored pastel, with
its bright red chairs set off against the

variegated greens of the trees and grass, reveals Shinn's increasing ability as a colorist. Instead of depicting a more conventional park scene in which people are shown quietly seated or walking leisurely on paths, Shinn has selected a dramatic moment loaded with energy. People are shown dashing for cover overturning chairs in their haste to find shelter from the storm, revealing once again Shinn's flair for the dramatic spectacle. It is likely that Shinn's experience in the Luxembourg gardens acquainted him with the artistic possibilities of such leisure spaces and when he returned to New York he approached Central Park with a broadened sense of compositional strategies.

In pictures such as *Bridal Path in Central Park* (c. 1920s; The Cheekwood Museum of Art)[168] and *Untitled (Park Scene)* (c. 1901; FIG. 3) Shinn focuses on the spectacle of the modern park. In *Bridal Path in Central Park* a group of riders is shown galloping through a secluded area of the park. During the mid- 19th century, equestrian sports were extremely popular across all classes, harness racing ranking as the leading spectator sport in America.[169] The procession of the well-dressed riders on Central Park's bridal trails was described in a contemporary review. The writer observed, "Early in the morning, in spring or autumn, these byways are alive with equestrians. Now a young woman, with a groom following dashes by you as you watch from the walk, or a party from a riding school charges down upon you like a troop of

cavalry and disappears around a turn, into the woods; occasionally a mounted policeman rides slowly by, man and mount alike alert for the not infrequent runaway."[170]

Upper class dominance of the park gradually gave way to a more socially diverse population. By 1907, the park's demographics had changed such that Henry James could write:

> I recall…during a couple of hours spent in the mingled medium, the variety of accents with which the air swarmed seemed to make it a question whether the Park itself or its visitors were most polyglot. The condensed geographical range, the number of kinds of scenery in a given space, competed with the number of languages heard, and the whole impression was of one's having had but to turn from the plaza to make, in the most agreeable manner possible, the tour of the little globe.[171]

Central Park's appeal to a wider audience is reflected in *Untitled (Park Scene)* (FIG. 3).[172] The picture is composed of zigzagging diagonal paths. In the foreground, a uniformed nurse wheels her charge in a perambulator past two fashionably dressed ladies who are out for an afternoon stroll. Other pedestrians contribute to the parade, which is observed by the equally mixed crowd of spectators seated on a bench. The scene is very close to that described by a writer for *Harper's Magazine* who made the following observations regarding those who frequented Central Park, "It is a democratic crowd, made up of all classes and conditions of life. Elegant men and women jaunty collegians, nurse-maids and their restless charges, German fathers of families, with the wife, babies, and grandmother all together in a crowd, young sweethearts arm in arm, forgetting that they are not alone in the world — all are there; fighting their way through the mass of people…"[173]

By selecting certain aspects of park life, Shinn found a way to make Central Park suitable material for his depictions of modern life. After 1901, however, his attention turned to Washington Square Park close to 112 Waverly Place, where the Shinns moved in 1902.[174]

Washington Square Park

Of the many picturesque locales in New York, none received the attention that Shinn lavished upon the park at Washington Square. He depicted it no fewer than 20 times from several angles and under various weather conditions, though he was certainly not alone in his admiration for the square. The park was popular with numerous artists, many of whom, like Shinn, lived on or near Washington Square.[175] Those who rendered the locale's rich visual history included Ernest Lawson, Edward Hopper, Paul Cornoyer, Guy Wiggins, and Childe Hassam. Interestingly, the two early twentieth century artists who created the greatest number of paintings and drawings of the square were Shinn and his close friend Glackens who moved to a studio at 3 Washington Square North in 1904.[176]

The Shinns' move to 112 Waverly Place was noted in *House Beautiful*, which featured their new home in the December 1902 Christmas issue. In an amply illustrated article, Charlotte Moffitt wrote approvingly:

> Mr. Everett Shinn, a clever artist of the brush and crayon, and Mrs. Shinn, with her precious heritage of Biddle furniture, pictures, and silver, have sought out this little setting in Waverly Place and made everything so harmonious that once inside, with the door closed

upon the noise and bustle of town, one is transported to the days of the fair women and doughty heros whose faces look down upon one from the walls.[177]

The house itself (which is still extant) is a quaint four-story brick structure with colonial doorposts and Doric cornices. The furnishings in the well-appointed home included a mahogany table and two gold chairs given to Shinn by Clyde Fitch. Sunlight filtered through Indian shawls draped at windows onto the walls adorned with Shinn's paintings. Shinn's studio was on the top floor, although he would later build a much bigger work-space behind the house.

Washington Square, which marks the beginning of Fifth Avenue, had once been a large Potter's Field. Officially opened as a public park on the July 4, 1828, the area was soon surrounded by exclusive private houses, the most notable of which were a row of town-houses on the north side of the Square. Built in the early 1830s this attractive line of Greek revival houses was much admired by Shinn who viewed it as an elegant reminder of an earlier era.[178] He observed, "There is nothing like it. The architecture of the row of houses is of the best — it is the only mark to be found in New York of a fine old city."[179]

The most prominent feature of Washington Square was the monumental arch built to commemorate the centen-nial of George Washington's inauguration as president. The arch fea-tured in Shinn's work is the second version of the arch. The first arch, built by Stanford White in 1889, was a tempo-rary wood and plaster structure, which proved so popular that White was enlist-ed to build a permanent structure. Structurally completed in April 1892, White's dazzling marble arch recalled majestic Roman arches and immediately became a source of civic pride and an inspiration to many painters.[180]

When the Shinns moved to the neigh-borhood prominent residents occupied the north side of the square, while the south side of the square was home to an Italian immigrant community. Here on well-shaded paths ladies and gentlemen could promenade, young people could gather, and lower classes could find respite in a pleasant environment. The park itself was a border effectively described by Mariana Griswold van Rensselaer who observed:

> A couple of miles up-town is Washington Square, where…there are many tramps,…a sprinkling of baby wagons and white-capped nurses; for this is the boundary-line between very poor and crowded and very well-to-do and roomy streets of homes — South Fifth Avenue, with its teeming French, German, Irish, and Negro

population, ending against one of its sides, and the true Fifth Avenue starting from another.[181]

The variety of people who frequented the Square appealed to Shinn and he was attentive to their interactions and to the demographic changes that occurred in the area over the years. In his notes on Washington Square he recalled:

For over fifty years I breathed the changes in Washington Square. Lifted to exhulted [sic] enthusiasm with some and gagged on others. Close at hand to where I lived it drew my interest, day and night to sketch, to look, or rest.

In 1900, the north side exuded a perfumed exclusiveness. A bastion, lined in unity against the uneasy bohemian spirit where the trancient [sic] dwellers of "genius row", thumbs to nose, gestured their distain [sic] for those who wrote their names for fame on checks for Opera boxes. Liveried coachmen held their reins over the glossy flanks of thoroughbreds at the curb before the stately pillared doorways that marked societies [sic] line of defence [sic].

Precice [sic] in dress, men attended the mincing steps of wives or daughters in strolls through the park's paths to doff silk hats in

recognition of their kind swathed in veils and tilting sunshades…

Slowly the southside edged its way, moving north like moths toward the gleam of chrystal [sic] chandeliers. Then the benches lost their ghost like sachet fragrance to the stronger scent of tramps…[182]

Never tiring of its artistic possibilities, Shinn always returned to it as a source of inspiration. He recalled:

It was after one o'clock when I left my door at 112 Waverly Place, scarce two hundred feet from the west side of Washington Square where I had hoped to find more material for sketches that would serve for factual data for larger paintings…Diversified material was always there. I had drawn it from every angle, in snow, rain, sun and moonlight, yet even the older and more selective spots seemed to come into freshening interest by the alchemy of changing seasons.[183]

In 1911 when the *New York Times* asked twelve artists "What is the Most Beautiful Spot in New York?" Shinn praised Washington Square. He explained:

Yes, when I want to be sure to find beauty I go to Washington Square.

Of course there are plenty of other fine spots in New York. But — when you want to be reasonably sure of getting a good meal, you prefer to go to your favorite restaurant, don't you?….Well the same sort of thing happens to me with Washington Square. No matter what the conditions may be under which I see it — no matter what my mood may be — I feel almost sure that it will appeal to me as beautiful.[184]

Representations of Washington Square bracket Shinn's career providing the subject for one of his earliest as well as one of his last pictures.[185] Though Shinn depicted Washington Square as early as 1899, his interest in the park was strongest after his move to the neighborhood in 1902. By 1903, he had portrayed the Square several times including *Washington Square, After the Rain* (c.1902– 03; PLATE 20), *Washington Square and Fifth Avenue* (1902; Private Collection), and *Washington Arch during Snowstorm* (c. 1902–03; Location Unknown).

Washington Square, After the Rain most likely shows the square in late autumn as all but a few reddish leaves have fallen from trees. The viewpoint is from the south side of arch looking north toward the elegant line of Greek revival buildings that Shinn so admired. Evincing Shinn's remarkable skill at depicting weather conditions, the pastel effectively conveys

the blusteriness of the day. Above, the rain clouds are lifting to reveal a bit of blue sky. The pavement, still wet from the rain, glistens with the dazzling reflections of the red buildings, trees, arch, and carriage. The three accounts of the square were included in Shinn's exhibition at M. Knoedler & Co. in New York on view from March 9 to 21, 1903. A reviewer offered the following laudatory remarks regarding *Washington Square, After the Rain*:

[T]here are as well quiet tones of gray in sketches of this city seen under lowering skies, the sad and dreamy aspect of the poorer quarter, or perhaps such a corner as North Washington Square, with the art keyed low, upon a rainy afternoon. This last is an ambitious composition, excellent in its architectural drawing and effective in the contrasts between the red brick houses and the white of the marble arch, reflections being everywhere and by reason of the rain…[186]

Also included in the exhibition was *Washington Square and Fifth Avenue*, which presents the arch from Fifth Avenue, where, placed in the middle ground, it acts as a dignified portal to another section of the city. In the background, at the right, is the tower of Stanford White's Judson Memorial Church and to the left is an elegant town house marking the beginning of the stately row of houses on the north side of the Square. The restrained palette of ochre, green, and russet brown highlighted with white gouache is fitting for Shinn's dignified treatment of the patrician setting north of Washington Square.

A portion of the M. Knoedler & Co. exhibition was scheduled to travel to Chicago. In anticipation of the event, a Chicago critic reviewed the exhibition for his home audience. The article was accompanied by an illustration of *Washington Arch during Snowstorm*, which shows the similarity of this picture to *Washington Square, After the Rain*. Both works portray the south side of the arch looking towards Washington Square North. However, in *Washington Arch during Snowstorm* Shinn zooms in more closely on the arch, cropping the view on either side, so that the arch fills majority of the composition. The critic remarked:

> Admirable and delightful are several views of New York streets. Among them are three or more of the stately Washington Arch under varied atmospheric conditions. As in the view reproduced [*Washington Arch during Snowstorm*], for example, the beautiful structure set against a leaden sky, the snow blowing in all directions, blinding the eyes of the cabmen and horses, the people that are struggling to cross the square — the picture [is] mostly in black and white, the row of red houses in the distance enlivening the scene."[187]

The reviewer continues by noting that *Washington Square, After the Rain* presents the arch "again, almost from the same viewpoint as described at the end of a misty day the sunlight illuminating the brilliant red façades, the wetness of the street, the arch and trees rendered with much skill."[188] And of *Washington Square and Fifth Avenue* he remarks, "Here, too, is a view of the same subject from Fifth avenue on a rainy spring day, a picturesque old-fashioned house covered with green vines forming an important feature of the composition."[189]

Occasionally, Shinn would create two or more versions of a work, perhaps to replace a picture that had been sold or to experiment with a slight variation on the original composition. Two almost identical works are *Washington Square* (1910; Private Collection) and *Stormy Night in Washington Square* (c. 1910; PLATE 21). Both demonstrate Shinn's command of outdoor night scenes. In each picture the arch is set back in the composition and shown obliquely from the northeast side of the square. In the foreground, pedestrians huddle under an umbrella attempting to shield themselves against the wintry weather while a bicyclist struggles to navigate the snow-rutted paths. In the background, the electrically illuminated cross of the Judson Memorial Church is visible. The scene is bathed in both artificial illumination and natural moonlight, which not only unifies to composition, but also imparts an aura of mystery to the scene.

The two versions of Washington Square during a stormy night are not without differences. For example, the *Stormy Night in Washington Square* is cropped at the left and right and along the bottom edge. Also dissimilar are the number of foreground figures and the slight alteration in the positioning of figures that appear in both pictures. *Stormy Night in Washington Square* is undated and it is therefore difficult to know which version came first. *Washington Square* was illustrated in the *New York Times* article "What is the Most Beautiful Spot in New York," and it is possible that the image's popularity inspired similar pictures. Indeed, in addition to the resemblance between *Stormy Night in Washington Square* and *Washington Square*, the composition is also related to *Washington Square, Stormy Night* (1951; Location Unknown, formerly in the collection of the University Club), which shows the arch from the same angle and repeats some of the same motifs included in the two depictions of the arch discussed above.

In 1912, Everett and Flossie divorced and Shinn left his beloved Waverly Place residence. Washington Square, however, continued to occupy his attention. Even during the 1920s, when Shinn's creative energies were primarily spent on portrayals of the theater and illustrations, he produced at least one picture of Washington Square. *The Arch, Washington Square* (1929; PLATE 22) represents Shinn's only located Washington Square

picture from this period. The composition is typical of Shinn's portrayal of the square showing it as a center of bustling activity. Horse-drawn buses, hansom cabs and pushcarts all share the public arena. In the foreground, lively figures are rendered in a few well-chosen lines and a bit of wash attesting to Shinn's great artistic skill.

Green Park

Following his return from Europe, Shinn showed seven European park scenes in his exhibition at Boussod, Valadon & Co. Of these, Luxembourg Garden images out-numbered London parks, which were represented by only two pictures — *Green Park, London* and *Afternoon, Hyde Park*. The subject of Green Park reappears seven years later in the pastel *Green Park, London* (1908; PLATE 10). The intimate scale of the work belies its powerful depiction of urban poverty. Representing Shinn's continuing interest in society's less fortunate individuals, the pastel showcases the city's poor and dispossessed. At the center of the composition a man in rumpled clothes with a peg leg sits on a bench under a tree. He is surrounded by a woman slumped forward like a rag doll and two other figures who lie asleep or unconscious against the tree. The harshness of the subject matter is echoed in Shinn's almost brutal treatment of the pastel chalk, which is applied in quick, jagged strokes. The work demonstrates that even in 1908, the year Shinn was showing his spectacular paintings of theater scenes in the exhibition of The Eight, he remained committed to representing the broad spectrum of urban life including the lives of less fortunate individuals.[190]

Urban Amusements: The Spectacle of the Streets

As Sylvia Yount has noted, Shinn had a special flair for drama. She writes, "his [Shinn's] contribution to the Ash Can group lies in his portrayal of the city as 'dramatic spectacle.'"[191] Shinn himself recognized the way in which disaster was transformed into dramatic spectacle. He remarked, "Crowds, like fruit flies suddenly appear from nowhere and into empty streets to form in packed hungry morbidity about a morsal [sic] of human incumbant [sic] pain. Devouring the sight of a human being that had suddenly gone horizontal."[192] In his depictions of fires, street accidents, and fights, Shinn makes space for the viewer to participate vicariously in the thrilling scenes featured in his pastels. Such works presented the public with the drama and diversity of city life and as such helped them to make sense of the complex heterogeneous world in which they found themselves.

Fire on Mott Street (1902; PLATE 23) is one of Shinn's most spectacular depictions of an urban conflagration, a subject that he began depicting in 1895 as an artist reporter for the Philadelphia newspapers.[193] The high number of fires Shinn covered caused him to comment, "After a while you got to know without thinking about it just how many men there were on a fire engine, what the equipment looked like."[194] In *Fire on Mott Street*, a conflagration in an immigrant neighborhood has drawn a crowd of spectators who gather to watch the fire's brutality and to observe the heroic efforts of the firemen. In the right foreground the prominent figure of a firemen turns his body diagonally, aiming his fire-hose toward the burning building. In so doing, he leads the viewer into the center of the battle where at least two fire engines are silhouetted against the red flames of fire. The cascade of sparks that fall like fireworks on the people and objects below highlights the drama of the scene. Shinn himself acknowledged the theater-like effect of the event writing: "Fire on Mott Street. The shriek of the fire engine always drew me from remote places. I was there when the fireman coupled the hose exempt from the huddled spectators by the grace of a reporters police badge I squeezed beyond the line privileged to feel the shower of sparks."[195]

The steam fire engine in *Fire on Mott Street* is a motif that appears in at least two other of Shinn's works. Although it was already somewhat outdated, for Shinn it was an object of great pictorial interest. Prominently depicted by Shinn in an illustration for an article titled "Modern Fire Fighting," the fire engine is shown being pulled through Union Square Park.[196] A similar fire engine also appears in the pastel *Fire Scene* (1899; Yale University Art Gallery),[197] in a composition that is closely related to *Fire on Mott Street*. Both pictures feature dilapidated buildings with grimy façades and broken shutters suggesting that the fires are occurring in one of the city's poorer neighborhoods. However, despite the similarity of the subject matter, the works elicit very different responses. In *Fire Scene* the calm sinuous lines of the fire hoses and the somber palette restricted primarily to white, gray and black with highlights of blue and red creates an impression of elegance and restraint. By contrast, the agitated line and intense yellows and reds in *Fire on Mott Street* convey a sense of urgency, evincing the artist's skill at conveying the immediacy of the disaster.

Fire on Mott Street is one of two depictions of fire scenes, which date from 1902. In the second picture, *Fire on Twenty-Fourth Street* (1907; The Cheekwood Museum of Art),[198] the enormity of the conflagration is reinforced by the number of fire engines present and the vast number of spectators who have crowded below to observe the event.

Like fires, fights were always sure to draw a crowd. Shinn, who was attentive to the dramatic possibilities of New York street life found in fights the elements of suspense, action, and violence that made the subject fitting for pictures of urban spectacle. In *The Fight* (1899; PLATE 24), an altercation has broken out in front of a saloon. One man has just given his opponent a solid punch in the jaw. The wounded man reaches out with his hand perhaps in an attempt to regain his balance, but he appears about to tumble backwards. A spectator who attempts to pull the fist-wielding pugilist in the other direction heightens the push-pull effect. At the right, a group of men has gathered, forming an audience eager to watch the event. Rather than attempting to prevent the violence, the crowd merely looks on, one man even smiling gleefully as if he were rooting for his team at a sporting event. Indeed, *The Fight* looks forward to the boxing pictures of George Bellows and may have appealed to a similar audience. As Marianne Doezema notes in regard to Bellows's boxing pictures, "These ferociously expressive paintings represented, among other things, the intensity of 'real life' and the liberal challenge to middle-class social conventions, as well as heroicized masculine hardiness."[199]

Shinn produced several pictures of the fight subject starting with a pastel titled *Fight*, which was on view from January 15 to February 24, 1900 at the Pennsylvania Academy before being shown at Boussod, Valadon & Co. beginning on March 20, 1900. In 1901, a work titled *Street Fight* was included in the annual exhibition of the Watercolor Club at the Boston Art Club where it drew enthusiastic reviews. "Mr. Everett Shinn has studied his Forain and his Steinlein to good advantage as his 'Street Fight' shows," wrote one reviewer.[200] A critic for the Boston *Transcript* provided a description of the work that appears to identify *Street Fight* as the same picture as *The Fight* (c. 1899; PLATE 24). The writer notes, "Here is a fight between two toughs in the street, witnessed with keen interest by a lot of ruffians…. Good work, well observed and independently painted."[201] Moreover, watercolors are relatively rare in Shinn's work at this time, making it unlikely that other works in this medium would have fit the description of *Street Fight*. Shinn pursued the subject of men fighting in *Spoiling for a Fight, New York Docks* (1899; Milwaukee Art Museum), and *Street Fight* (1910; Location Unknown), and even took up the theme of professional fighting in *The Wrestlers* (c. 1900; Location Unknown) and *Prize Fighters* (c. 1904; Location Unknown).[202]

Fights and fires were just two aspects of Shinn's representations of the spectacle of New York street life. The grand thoroughfares of Broadway and Fifth Avenue afforded numerous urban amusements and provided ample opportunity for public spectatorship. Shinn's pastels record his observations and interpreta-tions of activities such as window-shopping, matinee attendance, and dining out in restaurants that had recently emerged as new forms of leisure entertainment. Like the city's streets and squares, the entertainment sites were public spaces where people could absorb the new ideas. Robert Stern et al. in *New York 1900: Metropolitan Architecture and Urbanism, 1890-1915*, refer to the years 1890-1915 as "The Composite Era,"[203] a period characterized by economic expansion and consolidation. The era witnessed a proliferation of building and a new sense of public life succinctly described by a writer for *Scribner's* as: "the growth in New York of the spirit of society…that instinct whose manifestations distinguish a great capital from a great centre of population merely, and are to be observed less in drawing rooms than out-of-doors."[204]

Restaurants

During this period many restaurants were founded to meet the demands of an increasingly social New York public. Restaurants such as Mouquins opened in the theater district and establishments like Delmonico's relocated to even more splendid quarters following the move of fashionable society uptown. During the late 19th century, Delmonico's was considered one the most expensive and aristocratic restaurants in the United States. Originating as a wine and pastry shop, the establishment was purchased in 1848 by Lorenzo Delmonico. Under his guidance, the staff learned to provide efficient service and the food reflected the epicurean splendor of the finest European restaurants. The dining room was transformed into an elegant public space where civilized manners reigned and the ballroom became the choice place to hold receptions.[205] Originally located on 14th Street Delmonico's moved twice, first to Fifth Avenue at 26th Street as in Shinn's pastel *Café Martin Formerly Delmonico's* (c. 1899; Mint Museum of Art) where it remained until 1897, and then to Fifth Avenue at 44th Street, the site of the pastel *Delmonico's Fifth Avenue* (1904; PLATE 25).

Delmonico's Fifth Avenue features the restaurant's majestic new building seen through an atmospheric haze from across Fifth Avenue. On the opposite side of 44th Street the distinctive squat building with the rounded roof was a meat market owned by Henry H. Tyson. To the right of the meat market at 527 Fifth Avenue was Ye Olde Willow Cottage that sold "ye olde demon rum."[206] In the foreground several hansom cabs can be seen moving jauntily along Fifth Avenue. The restrained palette, highlighted with touches of white and light blue, and the soft feathery treatment of the pastel relates to another work from the same year, *Towards the El* (1904; Location Unknown). The two pastels feature radically different sections of the city. In contrast to the glamour of Fifth Avenue,

Towards the El portrays a narrow street lined with brownstones. In the background, the inclusion of the El indicates that we have moved off the city's most fashionable avenues. Both works with their limited tonalities and subtle treatment of the pastel may relate to the works of Whistler.

Downtown in the theater district, a much different type of restaurant could be found. *Mouquins* (1904; PLATE 26) shows the exterior of the well-known restaurant at 28th Street and Sixth Avenue that was popular with theatergoers. In contrast to the refined establishments of Delmonico's or Sherry's, which sought to emulate the expensive interiors of their patrons' own dining rooms, Mouquins was an example of the new Broadway restaurant that provided middle class diners with a splendid setting that they could not find at home.[207] Mouquins together with the Café Francis were popular meeting places for many of the artists who later formed The Eight. Ira Glackens noted that, "The Prestons, Robert Henri and his wife, all their friends, were often to be found at one or the other."[208] Indeed, Shinn himself confirmed that "it was at Mouquins that the crowd really became intimate."[209] Glackens celebrated the establishment in his now familiar painting *Chez Mouquin* (1905; The Art Institute of Chicago), in which James Moore, the proprietor of the Café Francis, is shown with a female companion. Shinn's pastel, *Mouquins* which predates Glackens's *Chez Mouquin* by one year, shows the outside of the restaurant framed by the tracks of the Sixth Avenue El.[210] The exterior view is typical for Shinn, who was almost always more concerned with the street-life going on outside a noted establishment, than with the activities within.

The Promenade

Broadway is the one idling showplace. Neither the Strand nor the Boulevard des Capucines can replace it. Fifth Avenue is all that it should be — the one really perfect show street in the world.

— Theodore Dreiser, *A Traveler at Forty* (New York: The Century Co., 1915), p. 512.

At the turn of the century, Broadway and Fifth Avenue provided a kaleidoscope of visual display. People marveled at the new theaters, hotels, and restaurants that marked the changing urban landscape. Of particular interest to Shinn was the parade of people and carriages that crowded the city's major thoroughfares. The transformation of Fifth Avenue into an urban spectacle is aptly described by a writer for *The Architectural Record* who remarked:

Among the many radical changes which have been brought about during the past six years in New York City, the most radical and the most significant are those which have taken place on 5th Avenue.... It has been transformed in terms of human spectacle it presents by a great increase in the number of pedestrians. From being a comparatively quiet avenue....It has become a bustling thoroughfare, jammed with carriages and motors, crowded with shoppers and passers by, and redolent with the fumes of wealth and business.[211]

As the rich promenaded on foot or contributed to the elaborate processions of carriages, the middle class also took to the streets. As Mariana Griswold van Rensselaer observed of the public life of the middle class:

These people, and many others with small incomes who do not have homes of their own (but most often in cramped, inhospitable flats), find their amusement in theaters and restaurants, and the motley pageants on the streets, or, if more soberly minded, in concert and lecture-rooms and at church entertainments.[212]

Without purchasing a theater ticket or a meal, one could be well entertained on Fifth Avenue or Broadway. The streets provided free amusement in the form of window displays, cock fights, outdoor stalls, processions of well-turned-out shoppers and theater attendees, and parades. At the turn of the century a

Fifth Avenue event that was always sure to draw crowds of onlookers was the Easter Parade. On Easter Sunday men, women, and children dressed up in their Easter finery and paraded up Fifth Avenue on their way home from church. In addition to the numbers of people who participated, many more came to observe the spectacle. By 1905 the number of spectators had grown to such an extent that a writer for *Harper's Weekly* commented, "The truth is that the tradition has pretty well wrecked the show. On upper Fifth Avenue it is somewhat too dense now either for beauty or comfort. Such a vast number of people come on Easter to see the Fifth Avenue churchgoers walk home from church that the Avenue in the fifties begins to look and feel like Park Row at five o'clock when the Brooklynites begin to feel for the bridge entrance." The writer emphasized the theatrical nature of the parade observing, "When the audience flocks onto the stage in such masses as to impede the actors, it is bound to impede the performance, and something like that has happened to the Fifth Avenue Easter Parade. The obstreperous population of Manhattan, plain people and pretty, pious people and folks quite disinterested in piety as about raiment, gravitating out of enormous superabundance towards a much heralded free spectacle, have captured the Avenue and swamped the show."[213]

The pageantry of the Easter Parade appealed to Shinn and he pictured it several times, in illustrations that appeared in *Harper's Weekly* and *Scribner's Magazine* and in the intimate work, *Easter Sunday, Saint Patrick's Cathedral* (1900; PLATE 27).[214] In *Easter Sunday, Saint Patrick's Cathedral* the viewer's attention is drawn to the elegant carriage in the foreground with its two upright coachmen and finely dressed female passengers. The actual parade participants have been reduced to a colorful line of background figures rendered in quickly drawn lines of pastel and dabs of gouache. The entire spectacle is presented before the dramatic backdrop of Saint Patrick's Cathedral. The pastel is strikingly similar to the Easter Sunday illustration published in *Harper's Weekly* in 1900, and in fact the pastel may have been a study for the more elaborate representation.

Just Looking: Shinn's Shop Windows

Shopping was another aspect of the modern experience that captured Shinn's imagination. As Alan Trachtenberg has stated in his seminal work, *The Incorporation of America*, in the late 19th century urban industrialization led to the expansion of the marketplace. Mass production created a surplus of goods for which desire needed to be generated. Advances in technology and industries changed a woman's role from one who makes things to one who shops for things. Trachtenberg notes that by the 1890s, the word consumption had been redefined from its previous meaning of destruction to "all those desirable things which directly satisfy human needs and desires."[215] Trachtenberg locates the major site of consumption in the department store, which altered the urban space by attracting women downtown. The newly developed shopping district began on Eighth Street and followed Broadway to 34th Street. At 14th and at 23rd Street it turned west until it reached Sixth Avenue and included the stretch of Sixth Avenue between these two intersections. At the point where Broadway crosses Fifth Avenue the shopping district ran up Fifth Avenue until 47th Street.[216]

In Shinn's several pictures of female shoppers, the women are either shown out on the street amongst bustling crowds as in *Sixth Avenue Shoppers* (c. 1903; Santa Barbara Museum of Art) or staring into shop windows as in *The Shop Window* (c. 1903; PLATE 28)[217] Unlike Glackens who in *The Shoppers* (1907; The Chrysler Museum of Art) portrayed his wife Edith, her friend Lillian Travis, and Shinn's wife Flossie inside a store being attended by a clerk, Shinn did not generally venture inside establishments to depict his subjects. It is a curious and most likely unintended phenomenon that Shinn tended to depict the exteriors of restaurants such as Mouquin's or shops such as those featured in *The Shop Window*, while his close friend Glackens painted the interiors of the same or similar establishments.

Window Shopping (1903; FIG. 4) and *The Shop Window* are Shinn's earliest examples of shopping pictures, a theme to which he would return later in his career. Shinn may have appreciated the way shop windows, like the vaudeville stage, created a fantasy space that functioned also as a site of cultural exchange. Moreover, he may have been drawn to the "modernity" of the shop window, which had only recently come into being, the result of new technologies that made possible the production of plate glass, colored glass, and electric light.[218] The new materials reconfigured the domain of the theater and shop window by producing dazzling visual effects. Items for sale were showcased and dramatically lit attracting customers as if to a Broadway stage. As Wolfgang Schivelbusch, a scholar of the industrialization of light in the 19th century, commented on the changing landscape of the metropolis, "The illuminated window as stage, the street as theater and the passers-by as audience — this is the scene of big city life."[219]

Prior to 1890, the idea of the shop window display did not exist. Windows were used to light shop interiors and if goods were placed in them, they were generally pushed together in unappealing piles. The person who did the most to revolutionize window display was L. Frank Baum, who was not only the author of *The Wizard of Oz*, but also a fan of technology, particularly electricity, as well as the manger of a chain of theaters. In 1897, he brought his creative interests to bear on the new field of window design with the founding of the magazine *Show Window*. As William Leach has noted in his excellent essay on this topic, "Baum raised the status of the show window to the first place among advertising strategies. He advised retailers to have larger windows and to deepen them, to install wooden scenic backgrounds, and to stretch out the glass surface as far as it would go…. Baum advocated spectacular windows. Architectural displays, and devices intended not so much to display goods as to attract attention."[220]

Shinn was probably impressed by the way shop windows "opened up" public space. Prior to window displays, goods were "hidden" within the depths of intimidating shops. The window display solved this problem as it allowed "men and women, preys to that timidity which poverty in great cities brings, who are afraid to go inside and look at that which, seen from the outside, becomes an education to them."[221] Shinn likely recognized the seductive power the shop window not only to sell goods, but also to serve a pedagogical function by educating a disparate public as to the type of clothing popular with New Yorkers and how it was to be worn. When Dreiser's Sister Carrie arrives in Chicago, she is acutely aware that her clothes mark her as different from the other women. Studying the shop girls she observes, "Their clothes were neat, in many instances fine, and whenever she encountered the eye of one, it was only to recognize in it

a keen analysis of her own position — her individual shortcomings of dress and that shadow of *manner* which she thought must hang about her and make clear to all who and what she was."[222] Like Carrie, many new arrivals to the city wanted desperately to conform to their image of the well-dressed women. Display windows introduced inexperienced shoppers to fashionable clothing while at the same time they allowed women to avoid potentially embarrassing encounters with shop clerks to whom their unfamiliarity with the situation might be revealed.

[FIG. 4] *Window Shopping*, 1903
Pastel on paper, 15 x 19 inches
Private Collection

Window Shopping and *The Shop Window* are two striking examples showing encounters of female shoppers with modern window displays.[223] The pastel *Window Shopping* (FIG. 4) portrays a night scene in which the rain soaked street is illuminated by the bright artificial light of the window display. The window has caught the attention of an elegantly dressed lady who has stopped to gaze at the fashionably clad mannequins in the window. Mannequins were a new feature of turn-of the-century advertising. Early mannequins were primitively made, many without heads and arms, but by 1900 they had become authentic looking replicas of human beings.[224] Shinn's picture presents a humorous encounter in which the mannequins in their magical display window seem to have come to life. Mimicking an encounter between actual pedestrians on the street, the mannequins are seemingly startled by the intrusion of an outsider into their space.

Window Shopping is clearly one of Shinn's most theatrical street scenes. Positioned like actresses on stage, the mannequins stand bathed in incandescent light. Their elevated window box has become a mini-stage, recalling the words of a contemporary writer who observed, "The shop-windows, with their elaborate displays, their free exhibitions of the fashionable and the beautiful, are never without their crowds about them."[225] Like the vaudeville theater, the shop window provided a space where the spectator could encounter new ideas and "typical" American customs. The process of acculturation was facilitated by the introduction of mannequins, which exerted a powerful influence on public perception because people could identify with them. As Leach writes, "Female mannequins were perhaps the most radical display fixtures ever to appear in the store window. They helped transform the character of the public female image."[226]

The encounter of a female pedestrian with an enticing display window is also the subject of the pastel *The Shop Window* (c. 1903; PLATE 28). The exhibition of colorful stockings on mannequin legs is echoed in the gesture of the window shopper herself who lifts her skirt to expose a bit of light blue stocking. As fashion historian Valerie Steele points out, even before the turn of the century when luxurious lingerie became fashionable, colorful embroidered stockings were a provocative, but acceptable complement to street clothing.[227] Shinn has either cleverly created his own imaginary window display of stockings or emulated an actual one that appealed to him. Again the presentation of the window is stage-like. The stockings are shown on mannequin legs that are provocatively featured as if they were being thrust out from under a rising curtain. The colorful bolts of cloth to the left and right of the stocking-clad legs act as curtains being drawn back for the performance. Below, the swath of yellow entablature emulates the bright footlights of Shinn's theater pictures. As in the theater, the onlooker is invited to enter the realm of luxury (here in the form of silk stockings), of infinite possibility. Indeed, as one retail promoter advised, "Sell them their dreams, visions of what might happen if only.... After all, people don't buy things, they buy hope."[228]

The shopping district drew large numbers of women who came to the area to spend time and money. Like shopping, matinee theater attendance became an acceptable activity that a woman could indulge in without a male escort. Enterprising theater owners capitalized on the advent of the female shopper by building their establishments on the main shopping streets where they could appeal to women who had come to visit the stores.[229] By 1899, the area was packed with theaters. Daly's Theater, the Broadway Theater, Wallack's Theater, the Casino, Manhattan Theater, and Bijou Theater were just some of the performance houses situated on Broadway. The crowd of people who gathered on the street before and after the matinee provided yet another opportunity to look and be looked at. As Dreiser's Carrie remarked, "The walk down Broadway, then as now, was one of the remarkable features of the city. There foregathered, before the matinee and afterwards, not only all the pretty women who love a showy parade, but the men who love to gaze upon and admire them."[230]

The matinee crowd on Broadway is the subject of *Broadway, Late in the*

Afternoon, After the Matinee (1899; PLATE 29). The picture displays Shinn's skill at rendering the frenetic activity on one of New York's busiest and most important thoroughfares. Hansom cabs and pedestrians seem near to colliding as other figures jostle each other for space. On the left-hand side of the pastel a woman wearing a white fur collar and long bustling skirts makes her way across the busy street. On the other side of the street men turn their heads to stare and one leans forward perhaps to catch a glimpse of the lady whose face is obscured by the snow-covered umbrella. The lady with a white fur collar and billowing white skirt, who has probably just been to the matinee, strides purposefully down Broadway unaware that she has caught the eye of a male spectator.

The pastel is an excellent example of Shinn's unique sense of composition and drama. Both in terms of style and subject the work relates to one of Shinn's other great interpretations of Broadway, *A Winter's Night on Broadway* (1900; Location Unknown), which appeared as the first color center-spread for *Harper's Weekly* on February 17, 1900. The pastel depicts the bustling crowds on Broadway and was instrumental in helping the artist to break into the world of magazine illustration. To an even greater degree than *A Winter's Night on Broadway*, the pastel *Late Afternoon Broadway, After the Matinee* effectively renders the vitality of the city. Utilizing a rushing perspective in which the orthogonals sharply converge, Shinn creates a dynamic push-pull effect. The viewer's gaze, which is carried rapidly back in space by the strong diagonals, is then pulled toward the foreground by the forward moment of the carriages and pedestrians. Overall, the pastel is a tour-de-force of public spectatorship capturing the parade of urban display that transpired on the city's streets as well as the curious stares and glances that it provoked.

The spectacle of the well-dressed lady walking unaccompanied in the city was cause for some men to stop and stare without shame. The phenomenon of people caught looking at other people drew the attention of not only Shinn, but also a host of photographers and painters. For example, the Byron Company, whose thousands of photographs of New York document almost every aspect of city life, created images that show men or young boys openly staring at the elegantly dressed ladies as they make their way along the city streets. In painting, representations of urban spectatorship are found in Hassam's depiction *Rainy Late Afternoon, Union Square* (1890; Museum of the City of New York) and Sloan's *Sunday Afternoon in Union Square* (1912; Bowdoin College Museum of Art). The pictures, however, differ from Shinn's in the nature of the interaction between the man/men and woman/women. In Hassam's painting, the male viewer appears more voyeuristic rather than merely curious as in Shinn's

picture. Moreover, the female being observed in Hassam's painting seems more vulnerable. She glances downward, her cautious steps a strong contrast to the self-assured strides of the woman in Shinn's *Broadway, Late in the Afternoon, After the Matinee.*

Broadway, Late in the Afternoon, After the Matinee received considerable attention when it was exhibited in 1901 at J. Eastman Chase's Gallery in Boston. One critic noted, "After the Matinee…with its stream of people pouring out of the theater doors into Broadway — suggests with marvelous and dramatic force the swarming life of the street, its movement and tumult."[231] Another reviewer noted the lady's independence in the public sphere. He recorded, "*After the Matinee* is a bewildering mass of carriages, horses, etc., in a snow storm. Out of all this turmoil emerges calm and collected the inevitable Gibson Christie Shinn girl, mistress of the situation as usual. Bus drivers curse and swear at each other, the elements howl above them all, but Miss Christie Johnstone prances along oblivious to all of them."[232]

Images of the Streets of Paris

It is useful to compare Shinn's images of Paris, which he continued to create from sketches long after his trip in 1900, with his New York City scenes. The pictures of French neighborhoods with their old buildings and winding streets are keyed to a different energy level than his representations of Broadway or Fifth Avenue. In contrast to his bustling, crowded representations of New York City, these works are surprisingly tranquil. For example, *Paris Street Scene #1* (1902; PLATE 30) and *Paris Street Scene #2* (1902; New Britain Museum of American Art) are characterized by a quietude unusual for the artist. In New York Shinn was attracted to the city's busiest crossroads, however in Paris he preferred the quaint old neighborhoods usually shown in the early morning before the streets were crowded by people. In *Paris Street Scene #1* a single figure makes his way down an empty street. The closed shutters and minimal footprints in the newly fallen snow suggest that we are seeing the city at dawn. *Paris Street Scene #1* and *Paris Street Scene #2* are possibly Shinn's first city scenes to be painted in oil, a medium with which he began to experiment shortly after his return from Europe. The paint is applied in thick broad strokes that effectively convey the impression of layers of snow. The paintings' intimate scale and restrained palette belie Shinn's confident handling of the oil paint.

Shinn first exhibited Parisian street scenes at Boussod, Valadon & Co. in 1901 where they were admired by critics who noted the pictures' change in tone. A reviewer for the *Brooklyn Daily Eagle* observed, "He has his serious moments, as shown in bits of picturesque old French streets or quaint corners not to be selected by the unartistic eye."[233] In 1903 Shinn showed a small group of the Parisian scenes at M. Knoedler & Co. Again the pictures' serenity was recognized by reviewers, one of whom seemed to breathe a sigh of relief upon finding a quiet moment in Shinn's work. Comparing the Parisian pictures to those of New York she opines:

> In all of these, [the New York City scenes] as in the river scenes, where impatient tugboats steam and jostle larger vessels bent on hurried errands, the restless spirit pervades. Mr. Shinn strikes his first note of peace in the Paris street scenes, his most recent works, and in so striking gains inconceivably in art and loses nothing in character and the absolute sense of locality which is his strongest gift.

> Of these handsome, low-toned and quiet canvases there are five or six examples, the most notable being "Late Afternoon, Paris," "Paris Rooftops" and "Winter Night, Paris." In all of these Mr. Shinn makes his strongest claim to his place already won in contemporary art.[234]

The critic's approbatory response to Shinn's views of Parisian streets likely encouraged his continuing interest in the subject. In 1910, he created one of his most elegant examples of the subject, *Paris Street Scene, Winter* (1910; PLATE 31). The pastel shows a quaint Parisian street covered by a blanket of snow. The pinks, grays and yellows of the apartment buildings harmonize with the violet of the sky. The area is quiet but for a figure standing at the left and two pedestrians headed down the windy street about to disappear around the corner. Despite the wintry weather, the people are not shown struggling against the elements as they are in Shinn's New York pictures (see for example *Horsedrawn Bus;* PLATE 6). Rather the figures move gracefully with an ease that belies the inclement day.

Depictions of the Theater, Café Concert, and Circus

Shinn's portrayals of the theater provide some of his most visually spectacular and sociologically complex pictures and reveal his life-long fascination with the stage.[235] Moreover, the theater scenes can be interpreted as representing Shinn's understanding of the way new forms of theater (i.e., the cleaned up version of Vaudeville that became popular at the turn of the century) provided a socializing effect on the city's incredibly diverse population. In his depictions of the French café concert, the English music hall, and the American vaudeville stage, Shinn explores the interaction between the performers and the audience and examines the way the performances united disparate crowds of people through humor and by providing a common sense of awe and wonder. By focusing on the reaction of the spectators as they are confronted with the new, unusual, and modern Shinn created images in which people could recognize themselves in their encounters with the complexities of the modern city.

Shinn's involvement with the theater went beyond the role of mere observer. He was an active participant in his own productions and was on friendly terms with several actors and actresses including Julia Marlowe whom he depicted in one of his earliest theater pictures, *Broadway Theater: Julia Marlowe in Barbara Frietchie* (c. 1899–1900; PLATE 32).[236] Around 1910, after receiving a commission to paint 22 x 45 foot murals for Trenton City Hall, Shinn built a large studio behind his Waverly Place residence. The studio also doubled as a theater that included crimson curtains, a proscenium, and a perfectly equipped miniature stage. Home to "The Waverly Street Players," an amateur theater group, which included the Shinns, the Glackenses, Jimmy Preston, and David Belasco's assistant, Wilfred Buckland, the theater had the character of a private club for friends. Admission was by invitation only. For the performances, Shinn wrote three four act melodramas: *The Prune Hater's Daughter, More Sinned Against than Usual*, and *Wronged from the Start*.

Early Representations and Reviews

Representations of the theater were first exhibited in 1899 when Shinn showed *Scene — Julia Marlowe, Fourteenth Street Theater*, and *Interior Keith's* at the home of Elsie de Wolfe. The following year he exhibited five portraits of theater personalities: one of De Wolfe, three of Julia Marlowe and one of Clyde Fitch and four theater scenes: *The Theater, Fourteenth Street Theater, The Lime Light*, and *During the Biograph* in his large exhibition at Boussod, Valadon & Co. One of these pictures caught the eye of a reviewer who commented, "...in a very dramatic way, he depicts a solitary figure on stage, with a vast empty background, and a darkened house, whose only illumination is the footlights."[237] *At the Hippodrome* (c.1900; PLATE 33) with its monochromatic palette and view of a distant, lone performer in a darkened interior is in keeping with these early accounts of the theater. Indeed, *At the Hippodrome* may be one of Shinn's earliest located theater scenes. Presenting a dramatic view of the theater's sweeping balconies, the work conveys the grandeur of the stage setting and the

curiosity of the foreground spectators who lean forward over the railing to view the performance.

Shinn's fascination with the theater was encouraged by his trip to Europe in 1900. In Paris and London he had the opportunity to examine the theater pictures of Degas and Manet firsthand. He also would have experienced the excitement of the café-concerts and the music halls as is evident in his subsequent depictions of such locales. The impact of Shinn's European trip is immediately manifest in the 1901 spring exhibition at Boussod, Valadon & Co. One is struck by the new emphasis on theater scenes. Indeed, a critic reviewing the exhibition remarked, "Two of the best studies that he showed last year represented the interior of theaters; there are many more of the same kind here."[238] The large number of stage scenes included his 1901 show reveals an artist who is clearly "stagestruck."[239] Of the 46 catalogued works, 12 were theater scenes. Shinn's record book also lists 39 works that were included in the show but not catalogued of which 17 represent theater imagery. Parisian music halls, theaters, and café-concerts are represented in numerous pastels such as *Back Row, Folies Bergères*; *Grand Ballet*; *The Bal Bullier*; *Ballet Dance (Orchestra)*; and *Gaieté Montparnasse*. The exhibition was well reviewed with several critics remarking upon the merits of the theater scenes. A reviewer for the *Brooklyn Daily Eagle* wrote enthusiastically:

[FIG. 5] *The Hippodrome, London,* 1902
Oil on canvas, 26⅝ x 35⅜ inches
The Art Institute of Chicago, Chicago, Illinois

Ballet dancers and scenes in the ballet should be especially noted for their suggested motion. Public shows of all sorts, such as punch and judy shows, wrestlers and dancers on platforms above the heads of the assembled crowd, are favorite topics. These are portrayed graphically in night scenes, with electric lights shining on the performers, while the people's dark forms in front make an effective foreground and setting for the principal figures.[240]

Degas's influence was also noted:

> The ballet girl has in Degas no keener and more interested observer than Everett Shinn. He manages to draw her with a little more mercy than Degas, as a fleeting form, which is not angles, splay feet, and stiff petticoats, but suggests the curves of the reasonably youthful human figure. It is in the scenes of café and cabaret and other public life, especially at night, that Shinn has caught best the impression Paris leaves on unjaded eyes.[241]

In March 1903 Shinn held a major exhibition titled "Paris and New York Types" at M. Knoedler & Co., where his theater pictures again elicited praise. Helen Henderson writing in the *Philadelphia North American* declared him "a modern of moderns." In particular she stressed the unusual viewpoint from which Shinn approached theater scenes, commenting that he portrayed "the artificial life of the folk at the cheaper theaters and concert halls, viewed always from behind the scenes." The prominent role played by the audience drew her attention and she remarked, "Of this novel view of [the] stage in its relation to the audience Mr. Shinn has made a special study."[242] Shinn designed the cover for the exhibition catalogue, which displays a lovely female performer wearing a long gown with her hair elegantly swept up standing attentively on stage as is awaiting her cue. The model was a favorite of Shinn's and she appears in at least two other pastels: *Bal Tabarin* (1902; Whitney Museum of American Art) and *Brella* (1902; PLATE 34).

By 1904, Shinn's exhibitions, though they were rarely held at the same gallery twice in a row, were annual events. As one critic observed, "Every year Mr. Shinn holds an exhibition of drawings in crayon and pastel at one of the galleries on Fifth Avenue: this year he has three-score and ten of large and small pastels at the Durand-Ruel Galleries..." After noting the display of city scenes he concluded, "His great haunt, however, is the café chantant, or the small Parisian theater. Here he finds the exaggerated poses of singers and comedy men good material, using the footlights for strong contrasts on the faces and figures of performers and the shadowy parquet for the heads and busts of audiences and orchestra in the foreground."[243]

With each passing year the theater became an increasingly prominent motif in Shinn's oeuvre. In 1905, when he held his first exhibition of oil paintings at E. Gimpel and Wildenstein, theater subjects accounted for half the oils in the show. In 1906, he received a commission to decorate David Belasco's Stuyvesant Theater (now The Belasco) in New York, for which he created an elaborate mural scheme consisting of naked and semi-naked women representing allegorical figures. Shinn's interest in the theater

culminated in 1908 when he joined Henri, Sloan, Luks, Glackens, Prendergast, Ernest Lawson, and Arthur B. Davies in the landmark exhibition of The Eight at MacBeth Galleries.[244] Demonstrating the high esteem in which he regarded his theater pictures, all eight of the paintings Shinn selected to represent him in the important exhibition were stage scenes: *Gaieté Montparnasse*; *Rehearsal of the Ballet*, *The White Ballet*; *Leader of the Orchestra*; *The Gingerbread Man*; *The Orchestra Pit*; *Girl in Blue*; and *The Hippodrome, London*. Shinn sold *Girl in Blue*, now titled *Revue* (1908; PLATE 48), from the exhibition to the illustrious patron Mrs. Harry Paine Whitney for $300.[245]

American Vaudeville and Variety Theater — The Audience

The people who frequented music hall and vaudeville performances provided Shinn with a lively heterogeneous crowd whom he depicted from various angles and perspectives. Theatergoers are shown in expensive boxes, in the stalls, from the stage wings, and directly in front of the stage silhouetted against the footlights. Fascinated by people caught in the act of looking, Shinn features the audience members not only watching the performance, but also observing each other.

One of Shinn's most striking accounts of a theater audience is *The Hippodrome, London* (1902; FIG. 5). First opened as a circus in January 15, 1900, the Hippodrome eventually became a music hall.[246] Shinn would have had the opportunity to visit the establishment during his trip to London in the summer of 1900 where he likely made many sketches for the finished painting. The work is one of Shinn's first large oils and its sure paint handling and visual force represent a startlingly rapid proficiency in the media. By lushly applying oil paint in broad confident strokes Shinn not only creates a sense of spontaneity, but also suggests the wonderful textures of the women's wraps and dresses.

In *The Hippodrome, London*, Shinn reverses the traditional vantage point — we are looking not at the stage, but at the audience. In pictures like this one, Shinn demands the viewer's complicity by positioning him or her as if seated in an adjacent balcony peering at the mass of spectators across the way. At the upper right, the trapeze performer, dressed in a red bodice and white tights, swings daringly close to the spectators.[247] Although the ostensible subject of the painting is an aerialist, she is no match for the spectacle of the audience, which immediately captures the viewer's attention. Here as never before and seldom after, Shinn focuses on the clothing, movements, and gestures of the mass theater crowd. Forming a triangular composition, the crowd seems to surge forward fanning out until finally restrained by the diagonal barrier of the balcony railing. Only one member of the audience leans back to marvel at the act, while the others lean over the balcony to observe the audience below. One young lady sitting right of center stares provocatively out, linking the viewer with the scene.

The Parisian audience was also a subject that inspired Shinn. Completed one year after *The Hippodrome, London*, the pastel *In the Loge* (1903; PLATE 35) is a breathtaking example of Shinn's interest in spectators in what is most likely an elegant French theater. In contrast to the breadth of the audience shown in *The Hippodrome, London*, *In the Loge* presents a close-up view of a few female spectators whose rapt attention is completely absorbed by events not visible to the viewer. The work is one of the few examples in which Shinn focuses entirely on the audience, making its members the leading protagonists of the picture. Also remarkable is the way Shinn has delicately rendered the faces of the ladies whose youth and beauty are markedly dissimilar to a related picture, *Balcony of a London Theater* (c. 1903; Location Unknown), in which a disheveled and much less refined audience is made the primary subject of the work.

Both pastels may have been owned by the same collector, Mrs. Chauncey Blair. In his record book Shinn notes that a work titled *Balcony, Paris Theater* (probably the same picture as *In the Loge*) was sent to Mrs. C. J. Blair on May 29, 1903 and paid for in full by October 14 of that year.[248] A few months earlier, Shinn had sent Blair a work titled *London Gallery*, which she purchased for $200,[249] but later returned to the artist. Of the incident Shinn recalled:

> I sold several pictures to Mrs. Chauncey Blair….One, the companion in degradation to "Microbe Alley" was of a top gallery in a London music hall, the rail lined with toothless leering hags, bedraggled clothes, and drooping rain-matted feathers. Mrs. Blair liked this picture. Soon after its delivery in Chicago, I received her check and a letter begging me to allow her to exchange the London Gallery for another picture more agreeable for

her walls. In her letter she had written, "I like it but my husband will not tolerate it on the wall in the sight of our daughter." She trusted me and I sent in exchange a French flower stand

Blair's purchase a few months later of *Balcony, Paris Theater* may have been intended to make up for the absence of *London Gallery* with a more decorous theater picture.

Depictions of the audience in balconies, such as those discussed above, are much less common in Shinn's oeuvre than works that portray spectators on the main floor of the theater silhouetted against the bright lights of the stage. *Girl in Red on Stage* (c.1905; PLATE 36) is a prime example of this type of composition. Here a singer is shown before a colorful, freely painted backdrop, which in itself is remarkable for its abstractness. The view of the stage, however, is obstructed by the two fashionably attired female spectators whose silhouettes, made more the more prominent by their large elaborate hats, fill about two-thirds of the composition. Turning her head slightly, the woman on the left shows the viewer a glimpse of her sensitively rendered face illuminated by the glow of the stage lighting. *Girl in Red on Stage* may have originally been called *The Song — French Stage*, shown in 1905 in Shinn's first exhibition of oils.[251] The picture's design is comparable to that of *Gaieté Montparnasse* (1906; Albright-Knox Art

Gallery, Buffalo), in which a prominent female spectator competes with the performer for the viewer's attention.

The primacy Shinn afforded the audience, his attention to its poses and gestures, was by no means exclusive to him. As H. Barbara Weinberg has pointed out, "The American painters of modern life focused on the audience more often than they did the performer when recording urban entertainments."[252] What is unique, however, is the attention Shinn pays to the vaudeville theater as a democratic space akin to that of New York's public squares.[253] Acting as a microcosm of the modern city, vaudeville houses allowed people to mingle with, study, and imitate others whose social and economic backgrounds were very unlike their own. By gently enforcing rules, vaudeville managers "Americanized" people. Recent arrivals to Manhattan absorbed the social etiquette that was expected in New York City to become what Gunter Barth has called "City People."[254] Although other forms of performance, for example the opera and the ballet, also brought diverse groups of people together, they could not surpass vaudeville's ability to appeal to such a broad audience, and not surprisingly, it was the vaudeville theater that Shinn represented most frequently.

By 1900 vaudeville was America's unrivaled leader of entertainment.[255] Popular in the sense that it was "of the people," vaudeville struck a blow to the Victorian strictures that divided individuals by race, class, and gender. Vaudeville's success derived from its ability to offer something for everyone. As Robert Synder, author of *The Voice of the City: Vaudeville and Popular Culture in New York* explains:

> The genius of such shows lay in their ability to speak to a complex and infinitely varied audience. By the 1890s, immigration and industrialization had made New Yorkers a people of divergent nationalities, religions, races, and classes — all of them wrestling, it seemed, with the definition of the proper roles for men and women.[256]

Thus, the vaudeville theater provided a forum where diverse people could encounter new ways of thinking, speaking, and acting and thereby learn from one another. It was a remarkable context, which both celebrated ethnic identities and managed to unite people by encouraging the formation of common bonds.

The origin of the term "vaudeville" has received a number of interpretations. Douglas Gilbert, one of vaudeville's earliest historians, offers that "the word derives from the French Val de Vire (sometimes Vau de Vire), the valley of the Vire River in Normandy, where quaint and sprightly songs were sung."[257] Robert Synder elaborates on Gilbert's definition:

"Vaudeville" was originally a French term, referring to either pastoral ballads from the valley of the River Vire or urban folksongs: *voix de ville*, or "voice of the city." By the eighteenth century, 'vaudcville' meant entertainments of music and comedy. But vaudeville, as turn-of-the-century Americans understood it, was variety theater that entrepreneurs made tasteful for middleclass women and men and their families by removing the smoky, boozy, licentious male atmosphere.[258]

Shinn portrayed Vaudeville's roots in more boisterous forms of entertainment in *Bowery Music Hall* (1904; PLATE 37). Rendered with quick strokes of watercolor and gouache, the account conveys the raucous environment of a downtown music hall. The work may have been at least partially inspired by the café-concert pictures of Manet and Degas, for example, Manet's *Corner in a Café-Concert* (1878–79; National Gallery, London). The licentious nature of the bowery music hall and the fact that it served large quantities of alcohol probably discouraged Shinn from frequent attendance, nevertheless he appreciated the subject and later recalled:

> A Bowery Dance Hall — An expectant spot in entertainment was the close harmony of "singing waiters." "Sweet Adeline would come from shapeless orifuses [sic]

under the waxed span of "handle bar" mustaches. While on the packed floor to the tin pan thump of a tuneless piano bodies gripped close and whirled away in a determined gauntlet run of sharp elbows and buffeting cushioned hips…The "singing waiters" silent now moved among the patrons, breezing their rumpled stained aprons, bare armed with fists barnacled with frothy beer mugs. Bring your own instrument of musical torture, it will be welcomed or splintered over your head. The fraternal instinct is spontaneous here.[259]

An interesting feature of *The Bowery Music Hall* is the inclusion of the banjo. Thought to have been invented by a native of Virginia, the banjo played an integral role in the early days of variety theater due to its staccato rhythm and its portability. Shinn's inclusion of the instrument anchors the picture in the realm of early American musical entertainment.[260]

One of the primary forces on the Vaudeville circuit was Tony Pastor, who is credited with transforming Vaudeville from it pedestrian origins in dance halls, saloons, and grogshops into a form of entertainment suitable for women and children. He issued specific rules that banned alcohol, sexually suggestive double-entendres and profanity. Pastor established his theater in Union Square, an astute move that placed him in close proximity to the best shopping and other emerging forms of entertainment.

In general Shinn did not provide specific names of vaudeville house in the titles of his pictures. However, a few of his most well-known images such as *Keith's Union Square* (c. 1906; PLATE 50) and *The Orchestra Pit, Old Proctor's Fifth Avenue Theater*, (c. 1906–1907; Collection of Mr. and Mrs. Arthur Altschul) do identify the locations of the performances. Keith's Union Square was owned by B. F. Keith who vied for the title of "Father of American Vaudeville" with Tony Pastor.[261] In September 1893, Keith opened his Union Square house in a refurbished theater. In the spirit of Tony Pastor, Keith and his partner, E. F. Albee, sought to refine vaudeville. The theaters became known as the "the Sunday School Circuit." Keith encouraged proper conduct within his theater by placing a sign on the wall that read: "Such words as liar, slob, son-of-a-gun, devil, sucker, damn and all other words unfit for the ears of ladies and children, also any reference to questionable streets, resorts, localities, and bar-rooms are prohibited under fine of instant discharge."[262] It was not only the performers to whom Keith gave instructions on proper behavior. The audience too was taught the rules of theater etiquette. Patrons in one of Keith's theaters received cards with the following requests:

Gentlemen will kindly avoid the stamping of feet and pounding of canes on the floor, and greatly oblige the management. All applause is best shown by the clapping of hands.

Please don't talk during the acts, as it annoys those about you, and prevents a perfect hearing of the entertainment.[263]

Thus, Keith's theaters provided instruction in proper behavior to the middle class and working class.

Keith's chief rival was F. F. Proctor who founded a chain of theaters beginning with Levantine's Theater in Albany in 1880. Six years later he opened the Novelty Theater in Brooklyn and shortly thereafter the Criterion Theater, also in Brooklyn. In 1889, he built his first New York theater, the 23rd Street Theater, between Sixth and Seventh Avenues. Proctor's name became synonymous with continuous vaudeville, a concept he introduced in 1892 with the catchy jingle: "After Breakfast go to Proctor's, after Proctor's go to bed."[264]

A typical vaudeville bill consisted of eight acts. Generally a placard with a number would be displayed indicating the act's position on the bill. Shinn occasionally included these numbers in his vaudeville scenes, for example, *The Orchestra Pit, Old Proctor's Fifth Avenue Theater*, which displays the number 7.

The first act was referred to as a "dumb act" as it did not involve talking and therefore was less likely to be interrupted by the arrival of latecomers. Dumb acts included performances by jugglers, acrobats, and animals. The second act was meant to prepare the audience for the show and could be anything, for example, a man and woman performing as in the delightful watercolor *Theater Scene* (1903; PLATE 38). The third act "was to wake up the audience" and often consisted of a comedy team or magician.[265] A big name filled the number four position, while number five, which came right before intermission, was another big name meant to keep the audience excited about the show. The sixth act had to regain momentum but not overshadow the seventh and eighth acts. The seventh act was the most important. This was the "top" or "star" spot, the most coveted position on the vaudeville bill. The final act was meant to keep the audience talking about what a good show they had seen.

Frequently the final act was a dazzling performance by trapeze artists, which was sure to send the audience home titillated. Trapeze acts were a spectacle to which Shinn was particularly drawn and he rendered aerialists on numerous occasions, for example *Trapeze Artists (Proctor's Theater)* (1940; PLATE 39).[266] Shinn was a regular visitor to Proctor's first New York theater, the 23rd Street Theater, located at 141 West 23rd Street. This was the site where Proctor intro-

duced continuous vaudeville with acts running from 11:00 a.m. to 11:00 p.m. Completed in 1940, *Trapeze Artists (Proctor's Theater)* is a tribute to Shinn's involvement with the early days of vaudeville. Shinn described the work as, "…a trapeze act over the audience, Proctor's 23rd Street Vaudeville house. From my sketchbook from the early 1900's. The blindfolded man standing there is about to do a dangerous turn."[267] The pastel features the dramatically lit interior of Proctor's where a trapeze performer, having swung across the audience, appears momentarily frozen in the air before gravity sends him swinging back in the opposite direction. The summarily drawn crowd below looks up, mouths agape in awe, heads tilted back in wonderment. Not only did trapeze artists provide an exhilarating example of dramatic spectacle, but also because the acts did not rely on verbal communication they could appeal to an immigrant audience not yet proficient in English.

Trapeze Artists (Proctor's Theater) is closely related to *Over the Audience* (1940; National Gallery of Art, Washington) and *The Tightrope Walker* (1924; Dayton Art Institute). Completed the same year as *Trapeze Artists*, *Over the Audience* presents a female performer swinging on rings in a setting very similar to that of *Trapeze Artists* suggesting the possibility that both works were based on sketches of Proctor's Theater around 1900. *The Tightrope Walker* adopts the same format and focuses the viewer's attention on a performer clad in a tight-fitting phosphorescent costume high above the audience.

In any type of performance the audience is paramount, but in Vaudeville the audience is made a part of the show. Interaction between the performers and the audience was a strong part of the theater's attraction and actors would tailor their performances to the responses of the evening's particular group of spectators. One of the mainstays of vaudeville was the monologist whose topical jokes and gags related to current events and local news.[268] Shinn's picture, *The Monologist* (1910; Wichita Art Museum) features a rotund man with the typical props including umbrella, top, and chair attempting to establish a rapport with the audience.

Shinn's depictions of funny men also included examples from the London stage. In *London Music Hall* (1918; PLATE 40) Shinn draws on his experience watching English comedians to provide this lively account. Painted several years after his return from Europe, the work features a "Lion Comique," a type of funny man who, dressed up in a top hat and tails, entertained the theater audience with a combination of song and comedy.[269] The oblique angle of the composition, the dramatic footlighting, and the view into the orchestra pit all recall Degas, although the male comic was not a subject that interested him. Shinn may have seen prototypes for funny men in

the work of Walter Sickert who by 1888 had established a solid reputation as the painter of music halls. Indeed, *London Music Hall* is close in feeling to Sickert's *The Lion Comique* (1887; Private Collection), which like Shinn's painting, features a nattily dressed "swell" before an orchestra pit. While it is unlikely that Shinn saw Sickert's painting, he may have studied a reproduction of it that appeared in *The Yellow Book* in October 1894.[270]

Though the title of *London Music Hall* identifies it as an English scene, it should be noted that the representation does not differ greatly from the artist's treatment of American vaudeville performers, for example *The Actor* (1903; Private Collection) and *The Orchestra Pit* (1907; The Westmoreland Museum of Art).[271] In each picture, a comedian, dressed in long coat and a top hat, stands at the edge of the stage and communicates directly with the members of the audience and/or orchestra. Often an exchange that appeared as a spontaneous dialogue between a performer and the orchestra leader was actually a well-rehearsed act. Mary Cass Canfield, writing for the *New Republic* in 1922, described the spiel of the vaudeville comedian:

> He is…an apparent, if not always an actual improviser. He jokes with the orchestra leader, he tells…fabricated confidential tales about the management, the other actors, the whole entrancing world behind the

scenes; he addresses planted confederates in the third row, or the gallery and proceeds to make fools of them to the joy of all present. He beseeches his genial, gum-chewing listeners to join in the chorus of his song; they obey with a zestful roar. The audience becomes a part of the show and enjoys it. And there is community art for you…[272]

Although Shinn usually featured the audience inside the theater watching the performance, he occasionally portrayed spectators from a different position, as in *At the Stage Door* (1915; PLATE 41), a representation of people waiting expectantly to see a cherished performer. The work is a wonderful study in gestures and expressions. One senses the awe and tentativeness of the lady on the right who is about to pass through the stage door. The gentleman behind her is much less impressed, frowning like a disbeliever who doubts the talent of the star. Next comes a couple who appear whispering to each other, while behind them a distinguished looking man stands patiently waiting his turn. At the far left a figure stares out as if assessing our right to pass through the vaunted stage door. The use of shallow space and the frieze-like composition is related to illustrations Shinn created for *Harper's Weekly* around this time and it is likely that *At the Stage Door* was conceived as a magazine commission.[273]

The Dancers

Shinn's favorite performers to represent were female dancers. Like Degas, Shinn frequently depicted the dancer from the wings of the theater or from backstage. The choice of unconventional vantage points was noted by a critic who remarked, "Mr. Shinn has the knack for making the most expressive backs, and his figures, seen from the wings and facing obliquely the audience are full of suggestive possibilities."[274] Shinn may have adopted the view from the wings to give variety to his numerous pictures of dancers and he may have appreciated the way the unusual angle afforded the opportunity to describe the audience's reaction to the performance.

In general, Shinn did not identify the dancers or performers who appear in his representations of the stage, particular identity being subsumed to the overall spectacle of the theater. Typically Shinn preferred generic titles that identified the painting or pastel by the color or style of the dancer's dress.[275] Thus several accounts of performers bear titles such as *Singer in White at Piano* (1913; PLATE 42), *The Black Dress* (c.1945; PLATE 43), and *Girl in Yellow on Stage* (c. 1906; Private Collection). Shinn's thoughts on the identity of individual performers are revealed in his comments to R. H. Norton regarding his painting, *Concert Stage* (1905; The Norton Museum of Art). In 1940, Shinn wrote to Norton: "The picture you have is one of our

Vaudeville theaters in those days of smothering skirts. She has no particular identity. However, without fixing her on a known personality, she is, or the picture in its entirety is, my personality plus the forgotten vaudeville performer which inspired it."[276]

The most characteristic costumes for Shinn's dancers are long white or yellow dresses with ruffles along the skirt and puffy or ruffled sleeves like those represented in *Woman on a Stage* (c. 1910; PLATE 44) and *Paris Stage* (1907; PLATE 45). Typically the performer lifts her dress slightly with one or two hands in a lively fluid motion exposing a seductive bit of ankle. The motif of the dancer in white reached its peak in 1910 when Shinn created numerous variations on the theme. Works such as *Dancer in White Before the Footlights* (1910; retouched, 1952; The Butler Institute of American Art) and *Untitled, Dancer in White Dress* (1910; Location Unknown) both feature the artist's characteristic dancer in white shown from an oblique angle.

A French Music Hall (1906; PLATE 46) is one of the artist's most enchanting forays into the subject of the Parisian music hall. It is also an outstanding example of Shinn's treatment of dancers on stage presenting two gaily-dressed female entertainers who turn to greet the crowd. Through the use of color, Shinn artfully plays the two women off each other. The blond wears a white dress, the brunette a dark blue gown, a juxtaposition that

echoes the sharp tonal contrasts produced by the glare of the footlights.

The viewer is positioned as if seated in the loge behind the group of ladies at the lower left, a vantage point that clearly shows Shinn's indebtness to Degas.[277] As the art historian Robert Herbert has noted of similar views by Degas:

> This makes us into a spectator twice over. We look at the stage, but also at another operagoer...a complication of the viewer's role avoided by Cassatt and Renoir. In their pictures we are the traditional 'fly on the wall,' the viewer without a strong fictional presence, therefore we do not share with the figures the sight of the stage. The audience alone constitutes our spectacle. In Degas's loge views, we cannot disregard our imaginary presence.[278]

Our presence is further emphasized by the gaze of the lady in the audience who stares directly out at us.

In an early article on Shinn, A. E. Gallatin, an admirer and collector of the artist's work, illustrated *A French Music Hall*, noting the work's compositional relationship to the work of Degas. "But," he remarked, "Shinn has only gone to Degas for ideas, not to slavishly copy him. He has learnt to see things from Degas' point of view; he too now sees the artistic possibilities of the gaslighted music hall."[279] Referring to the Fraad picture Gallatin observes, "He has grasped and preserved the very spirit of these scenes for our edification. Very real they are: we might almost be looking in upon an actual scene."[280]

Linda Ferber in her article on Shinn's theater pictures has noted that the evolution of *A French Music Hall* can be traced to an earlier pastel, *At the Performance* (1903; PLATE 47).[281] Displaying a vivid palette of blue, green, yellow and white the work represents one of the finest examples of Shinn's early theater pastels. Like *A French Music Hall*, *At the Performance* affords a view of the interior of the music hall. To the left we glimpse a fashionably dressed couple seated in an expensive box. On stage a dancer in a white dress stands before the yellow swath of footlighting. The architecture of the stage is similar to that of *A French Music Hall*, as is the view into the orchestra pit. Both pictures also display a backdrop painted with a landscape, balustrade and urn, which became a characteristic feature of Shinn's stage scenes.

Shinn also depicted Spanish dancers in two of his most stunning representations of the subject *Spanish Music Hall* (1902; PLATE 49) and *Keith's Union Square* (c. 1906; PLATE 50). Around the turn of the century, Spanish dancers were enjoying great success in New York. One of the most famous, Carmencita, infatuated John Singer Sargent who threw parties for her in New York. In 1890, both

Sargent and William Merritt Chase painted Carmencita's portrait and her popularity even extended to the display of her dancing slippers in the back parlor of the Tenderloin Club, a New York meeting place for artists and writers.[282] The rage for things Spanish was still a force in the early 20th century. The opera *Carmen* was immensely successful and played repeatedly throughout the early years of the century. Mlle. Otero, a well-known Spanish dancer who was currently sharing the New York spotlight with Carmencita, caused a huge sensation when she arrived unannounced at the Tenderloin Club. A writer recalled:

> She wore her dancing-gown and over her head a filmy white lace Spanish scarf that emphasized her rich brunette beauty. Had she been evolved from the smoke itself the Tenderloiners would not have been more surprised. A space was cleared for her in the centre of the room, and she whirled in to the music of the band, performed one of the dances which were the rage at that time, and whirled out again. Before the spectators realized that the dance was over they heard from the street below the slam of her carriage-door, and the first woman guest of the club had gone. Mlle. Otero at that time commanded a higher price for a private performance than a grand-opera star.[283]

Shinn never visited Spain, but his enthusiasm for Spanish dancers may have been stimulated by Henri's descriptions of his trips to the Iberian continent that he began in 1900. Back in New York, Henri set about creating pictures of Spanish dancers using studio models.[284] Unlike Henri, Shinn probably based his Spanish dancers on performers that he witnessed in New York and Paris theaters. In addition to the general popularity of Spanish subjects, Shinn may have been attracted to the theme by the work of Manet whose Hispanicizing themes he would have recently seen in Paris. Paintings by Manet such as *The Spanish Ballet* (1862; Phillips Collection, Washington), *Lola de Valance* (1862; Musée d'Orsay), and *The Tragic Actor* (1865–66; The National Gallery of Art, Washington) evoke a sultry exoticism and drama that Shinn would later translate into his own depictions of dancers and performers on stage.[285]

In *Spanish Music Hall* (c. 1902; PLATE 49) a Spanish dancer, dressed in a brilliant yellow costume, is shown performing an energetic routine. She is one of the most spirited examples of Shinn's dancers, the torque of her body and the kicking up of one leg creating a remarkable dynamism. In the background sits a guitar player whose hat, boots and stance recall the Catalonian guitar player in Manet's *The Spanish Ballet*. The bravura brushwork and the thick, juicy handling of the oil paint is characteristic of Shinn's treatment of the medium from this point forward.

Keith's Union Square (c. 1906; PLATE 50) features a striking brunette dancer wearing a flowing white dress and red flower in her hair. Linda Ferber refers to *Keith's Union Square* as "one of several 'Spanish' song-and-dance motifs."[286] Shinn may have appreciated the Spanish dance for the rapport it invited between the dancer and the audience, who would become a part of the spectacle, clapping their hands, stamping their feet and crying out "Olé!"[287] Although in reality the Spanish dance could be quite racy, involving short skirts and provocative gestures, the dancers in Shinn's paintings, despite their lively movements, maintain a sense of decorum required of the vaudeville stage. Shinn may also have been drawn to the dancers' impressive costume. Such presentations of fancy dresses were popular with female shoppers who frequented the area around Union Square. Many women came to Keith's to see the costumes, which like the dresses shown in the shop windows, provided a wondrous spectacle of display.[288]

Shinn first exhibited a picture of a Spanish dancer in March 1904 when he showed the pastel *The Spanish Song* (Location Unknown) at Durand-Ruel Galleries.[289] In June of the same year he exhibited a pastel titled *French Theater, Spanish Song* (Location Unknown) at M. Knoedler & Co. In 1905, in his large exhibition at E. Gimpel & Wildenstein, were two oils of Spanish subjects, *The Spanish Dance* (possibly the original title of *Spanish Music Hall* or *Keith's Union*

Square) and *Carmen*.[290] *The Spanish Dance* was shown again at McClees Galleries in Philadelphia in 1907 and in 1908 Shinn exhibited *Spanish Dance, Music Hall* (possibly the original title of *Spanish Music Hall* or *Keith's Union Square*) at the National Arts Club in New York.

Shinn rendered his dancers primarily in either oil or pastel, however around 1906 he created at least two stunning accounts of female performers in red chalk. As has been already noted, Shinn was a strong advocate of red chalk utilizing it in many drawings of nudes and women dressing. In *Girl on Stage* (1906; PLATE 51), the red chalk is utilized with sureness and conviction attesting to Shinn's great skill in handling the medium. White gouache is used to form the swath of footlighting illuminating the dancer, bathing her in a sensuous incandescent glow and adding a brilliant immediacy to the picture. *Girl on Stage* is related to *Julie Bonbon* (1906-07; The Metropolitan Museum of Art) a red chalk drawing of a dancer, which in turn is related to a pastel of the same performer, *Julie Bonbon (The Stage from the Orchestra)* (1907; The Metropolitan Museum of Art). *Girl on Stage* and *Julie Bonbon* almost certainly feature the same attractive model who is shown poised and confident from a low vantage point as if we are seeing her from a seat in the orchestra pit.

Occasionally Shinn would portray a group of dancers on stage as in *Theater Scene* (c. 1906; PLATE 52), one of his most spectacular oils. The work is comparable to another of Shinn's masterful representations of the stage, *The White Ballet* (c. 1905; Collection of Mr. and Mrs. Arthur Altschul), which also features a stage packed with performers. As is typical of Shinn's stage pictures, *Theater Scene* clearly manifests the adoption of Degas's compositional strategies. The stage is shown from the point of view of a spectator seated in approximately the fifth row of the audience. The oblique angle and slightly raised position of the viewer afford a glance into the orchestra pit and across to the stage where a fantastic array of dancers perform in the glare of the footlights. Particularly remarkable is the painting's brilliant enamel-like color demonstrating the change in Shinn's palette from his earlier, more somber work.

Theater Scene, may have originally been called *Chorus in the Ginger Bread Man*. The Gingerbread Man, which in 1905 and 1906 played at the Liberty Theater in New York, was an elaborate production with a large cast that included courtiers, court ladies, chocolate éclairs, peasant girls, fairies and a chorus (FIG. 6). In 1906, Shinn exhibited an oil painting titled *Chorus in the Ginger Bread Man* at the Society of American Artists. The price for the work was $500 (the same amount that Shinn was asking for *The Hippodrome, London*) indicating that the picture was most likely large and considered important by Shinn.[291]

[FIG. 6] A scene from "The Gingerbread Man," the new musical play at The Liberty, Halftone photograph, nd, The Museum of the City of New York, Theater Collection

The reference to a "chorus" seems appropriate for the large number of performers in *Theater Scene* whose disparate characteristics and costumes do not appear to comprise a single act. Moreover, the fact that Shinn's oeuvre does not include many multi-figure stage scenes further suggests *Chorus in the Ginger Bread Man* as the original title of the work. In 1908, *The Ginger Bread Man* was included in the exhibition of The Eight.

In the 1920s, Shinn continued to create lively representations of the theater, a striking example of which is *Curtain Call* (1925; PLATE 53). On stage a male figure wearing a bright red jacket and matching pants accompanies a slender female performer clad entirely in white. She holds a parasol in one hand and extends her arms gracefully to criss-cross with the arm of her partner forming an undulating rhythmic line. The pairing of a male and female dancer is unusual for Shinn, who more typically preferred female dancers. Here he seems to appreciate the juxtaposition of opposites — male next to female and dark against light. Unlike his earlier more rounded figures, the dancers featured here are slender with long limbs, typical of Shinn's style at this time. Contemporary fashion favored tall, thin figures, a trend that is reflected in the illustrations that Shinn resumed following his divorce from Flossie in 1912 and continuing through his later work, including this painting. The background scenery is painted with a verdant wooded landscape recalling the style of Watteau or Fragonard. The palette is jewel-like, consisting of crimson red, emerald green, gleaming white.

The origin of *Curtain Call* can be traced to *The Vaudeville Act* (1902–03; The Palmer Museum; FIG. 7), which itself is a version (perhaps earlier) of a painting illustrated in the original exhibition catalogue of The Eight.[292] *The Vaudeville Act* is one of the artist's most animated representations of the vaudeville stage. The prominent, well-rendered performers and their placement on stage before a green, painted backdrop anticipate *Curtain Call*. One recognizes the red trousers and a white dress, but in the later picture the dress has been transformed into a delicate tutu revealing the dancer's long tapering legs. In *Curtain Call* the dance has also become livelier, evoking the spirit of the roaring twenties. Another significant difference is the absence of the orchestra pit. Beginning around 1910, Shinn started occasionally to crop the compositions of his theater pictures, eliminating the audience and orchestra pit in favor of a close-up view of the performers on stage.

[FIG. 7] *The Vaudeville Act*, 1902–03
Oil on canvas, 19 x 23 inches
Palmer Museum of Art, The Pennsylvania State University, University Park, Pennsylvania

The Circus

The circus had always been a major attraction for Shinn. His autobiography records his boyhood delight when the circus came to his home in Woodstown, New Jersey. As Shinn later recalled:

> Circuses were always the most wonderful thing in the world to me, and when a medicine man finally rolled into Woodstown on a single wagon my imagination was waiting for him, eager to be kindled. Dime store novels had laid the groundwork, like Indian scouts they had gone ahead of the circus and paved the way with scalps, feathers, bowie knives, tomohawks, fringed leggings, squirty cut plug, savage yells, hairbreath escapes, clowns and lurid greasepaint.[293]

In New York, he continued to visit the circus in Madison Square Garden and followed the big top when it traveled to Brooklyn.

Shinn first exhibited pictures of the circus at Boussod, Valadon & Co. in November 1901, showing *In Green Room Circus* and *The Circus*. His interest in circus subjects peaked in the 1930s and 1940s in his accounts of aerialists and clowns. *The Clown, (No Laughs)* (1935; PLATE 55) is an example of the amusing performers that attracted Shinn's attention on the vaudeville stage and at the circus. In the 1940s, Shinn found a ready market in California for his pictures of the circus, particularly clowns. From February 16 to March 20, 1947 he held an exhibition of circus and theater pictures at James Vigeveno Galleries in Los Angeles in which at least twelve of the pictures featured were of clowns.

The circus continued to fascinate him for the rest of his life. Shortly before his death in 1953, he took trips to Florida where he spent hours watching the Ringling Brothers Circus, making sketches for future paintings. In a letter to Miss Holzhauer at the Newark Museum Shinn wrote:

> I had had a wonderful time and made several sketches of circus life at the Ringling Circus headquarters and at the Ringling Hotel where the perfected acts were put on three nights a week for the hotel patrons. It's a great privilege to sit all directly under and very close to these performers...especially the man that balances himself on one finger. It does not seem like a trick.[294]

Epilogue

Everett Shinn died May 1, 1953 in New York Hospital of lung cancer. His obituary in the *New York Times* read: "A handsome and debonair man of many talents; Mr. Shinn will be remembered chiefly for his contributions to modern American art and for his role as one of the 'Eight Men of Rebellion,' of which he was the last survivor. He was an artist, sign painter, draftsman, engineer, designer, writer, composer, actor, teacher, carpenter, mechanic and theater impresario. In each role he sought the startling, the new and 'the natural.'"[295] Ironically, Shinn, who at the height of his artistic powers helped introduce America to daringly modern subjects executed in a spirited non-traditional technique, did not adapt to the changes in modern art. Although he showed in The Exhibition of Independent Artists in 1910, he ignored an invitation to contribute to the important Armory Show exhibition in 1913 and subsequently spoke derisively about modern art calling it "sneaking and malicious ... [art in which] Incompetence works to inflict slow death to healthy painting."[296]

Following his divorce from Flossie, he was married three more times, to Corrine Baldwin in 1913, Gertrude McManus Chase in 1924, and Paula Downing in 1933, each union ending in divorce. After 1913 his time was increasingly divided amongst various projects. He resumed his illustration career and accepted many decorative commissions for private homes and restaurants, such as the Oak Bar at the Plaza Hotel, for which he painted murals showing the area around the Plaza as it looked in 1900. Between 1917 and 1923 he worked as an art director for the motion picture industry where he was responsible for the movie sets of *Polly of the Circus* and *The Bright Shawl*. In 1943 he was made an Academician of the National Academy of Design, and in 1951 he was inducted into the American Academy of Arts and Letters. Although in his late work Shinn had largely drifted away from the verve and originality that characterized his early New York city scenes, in one of his last pictures, *View from New York Hospital* (1952; Collection of Mr. and Mrs. Arthur Altschul) he returned to the spirited rendering of the urban sphere that launched his career and evidenced his individual style in recording the spectacle of life.

Notes

1. This article was originally discovered in a scrapbook in the Everett Shinn Collection at the Archives of American Art [hereafter referred to as AAA], Smithsonian Institution, Washington, D.C. The collection, an invaluable resource for research on Shinn, includes correspondence, photographs, sketchbooks, illustrations, record books, and scrapbooks. There are six scrapbooks arranged by year on two rolls of microfilm. Scrapbook 1898–1906, Scrapbook 1910-1911, Scrapbook 1934–1924, Scrapbook 1934, and Scrapbook 1898–1952 comprise roll D179. There are also two undated scrapbooks on roll 952, frames 250-322. The scrapbooks contain clippings from newspapers and magazines labeled by Shinn with the source's title and date, but often missing the author and page number. For the above article see Scrapbook 1898–1906, roll D179, frame 46.

2. In the 1940s, Shinn began to write an autobiography that was never completed or published. Edith DeShazo, author of *Everett Shinn, 1876–1953, A Figure in His Time* (New York: Clarkson N. Potter, Inc., 1974), deposited most of Shinn's autobiographical material with the Everett Shinn papers at the Helen Farr Sloan Library, Delaware Art Museum, Wilmington, Delaware. The Shinn Autobiographical Material will hereafter be referred to as SAM in accordance with the abbreviation given to it by DeShazo.

3. Shinn does not specify which of the Mrs. Vanderbilts purchased his work.

4. Aline B. Louchheim, "The Last of the Eight Looks Back," *New York Times*, November 2, 1952, sec 2, p. 9.

5. Henri Pène du Bois, "Art Notes of Studios, Shops and Galleries," *New York American* (no date, probably March 1904), p. 34. Scrapbook 1898-1906, AAA, roll D179, frame 55.

6. Gunter Barth, *City People The Rise of Modern City Culture in Nineteenth-Century America* (New York: Oxford University Press, 1980).

7. Birth certificate of Everett Shinn, reproduced on stationary of The State of New Jersey, State Library, Archives and History Bureau with the notation: "The following has been correctly copied from a record of Birth formerly in the Division of Vital Statistics and Administration, now on file at the Bureau of Archives and History." A copy of this document is located in the Shinn papers, Helen Farr Sloan Library, Delaware Art Museum.

8. The author is indebted to Harold Shinn's step-daughter (who wishes to remain anonymous) for supplying biographical information about Harold Shinn.

9. SAM.

10. Letter of Vivien Shinn Thomas, New Jersey, to Edith DeShazo, New Jersey, 25 November 1973, Everett Shinn papers, Helen Farr Sloan Library, Delaware Art Museum.

11. DeShazo, *Everett Shinn, 1876–1953*, pp. 7, 9.

12. There is some confusion surrounding the year of Shinn's enrollment. In his autobiography, Shinn claims that he entered the Spring Garden Institute at the age of seventeen. This would make the year of his

enrollment 1893; an unlikely date as Shinn is known to have enrolled at the Pennsylvania Academy of Fine Arts in 1893. A more plausible date would be the end of 1890 or the beginning of 1891. This is based on the fact that Shinn spent two years at the Spring Garden Institute. One also has to account for the period he spent as an employee of Thackery Gas Fixture Works, making 1890 a plausible year for Shinn's enrollment. Bennard Perlman also notes that Shinn and John Sloan attended the Spring Garden Institute at the same time. John Loughery, Sloan's most recent biographer, cites autumn of 1890 as the date of Sloan's enrollment at the Spring Garden Institute, which would place Shinn there at approximately the same time. Unfortunately, it is not possible to check a student register at the Spring Garden Institute for the dates of Shinn's enrollment. After the Spring Garden Institute (later called the Spring Garden College) closed in 1992, the school's archives were lost or destroyed. Information on the Spring Garden Institute is based on correspondence between the author and Ted Taylor, author of *Spring Garden History*, (Philadelphia: Spring Garden College, 1975), on July 2, 1999 and July 9, 1999. Bennard B. Perlman, *Painters of the Ashcan School: The Immortal Eight* (New York: Dover Publications), p. 50; and John Loughery, *John Sloan* (New York: Henry Holt and Company, Inc., 1995), p. 14

13. SAM.

14. Everett Shinn, "Life on the Press," *The Artists of the Philadelphia Press*, (Philadelphia: Philadelphia Museum of Art, 1945), p. 9.

15. On October 16, 1945, Carl Zingrosser, curator of Prints at the Philadelphia Museum, wrote to Shinn asking whether Sloan, Luks, Glackens and Shinn had been employed on the *Press* at the same time. On October 25, 1945, Shinn responded, "About Sloans [sic] article where he says that 'Glackens had just stepped out of the Press when I came from the Inquirer.' That could be an all covering truth…yet…I still believe that all four of us one time sat together at the Press…Glackens I know went down to the Ledger and perhaps that is when Sloan came over to the Press…Perhaps I am wrong for I strongly believe that Glackens came back to the Press…The confusion is in me after all as I shifted from paper to paper and was after a few months on my rounds of the Press, Times and Inquirer." Shinn correspondence, Special Collections Department, Van Pelt-Dietrich Library Center, University of Pennsylvania, Philadelphia.

16. John Sloan, *The Artists of the Philadelphia Press*, p. 7.

17. SAM.

18. For Glackens's employment on the Philadelphia *Press* and his involvement with the Charcoal Club, see William H. Gerdts, *William Glackens* (New York: Abbeville Press, 1996), p. 12.

19. Mahonri Sharp Young, *The Eight* (New York: Watson-Guptil Publications, 1973), pp. 20-21.

20. "These Two Young Artists are Married, Happy and Proud of It," *News*, Baltimore, Maryland, undated clipping in Shinn papers, AAA, roll 953, frame 195.

21. SAM.

22. Loughery, *John Sloan*, p. 32.

23. Nina Kasanof, "The Illustrations of Everett Shinn and George Luks," (Ph.D. Dissertation, University of Illinois at Urbana-Champaign, 1992), p. 23.

24. John Sloan, *The Gist of Art* (New York: American Artists Group, Inc., 1939), p. 3.

25. Everett Shinn, "William Glackens as an Illustrator," *American Artist* (November 1945): 22-23.

26. Ibid.

27. Student Register, 1894-1904, The Pennsylvania Academy of Fine Arts, AAA, roll P62, frames 391, 402, 735.

28. Perlman, *Painters of the Ashcan School: The Immortal Eight,* p. 66. According to Shinn's marriage license, dated January 26, 1898, at the beginning of 1898, Shinn was residing at 145 East 21st Street. Marriage License of Everett Shinn, Philadelphia City Archives, Roll 1898 M 100020.

29. Everett Shinn, "I Remember New York," SAM.

30. The Shinns' marriage certificate is on file at the Philadelphia City Archives, Roll 1898 M 100020.

31. Two volumes of *Frederique* were published in 1907 by Frederick J. Quinby of Boston. Shinn was paid $700 for his 20 illustrations. The illustrations are listed in Record Book 1, pp. 70-71. Between 1899 and 1911 Shinn kept two record books, which provide invaluable information on the work of the artist. The first record book lists pastels, oil paintings, and decorative works sent to exhibitions and frequently includes information such as medium, price and purchaser of pictures, but unfortunately gives neither dimensions nor dates. The second record book lists illustrations submitted by both him and Flossie to various periodicals as well as some works sent to exhibitions. The record books, available on microfilm at the Archives on American Art, microfilm rolls 952-953, will hereafter be referred to as Record Book, no. 1 and Record Book, no. 2.

32. There are many books and articles on this topic. Amongst the most helpful are Wanda Corn, "The New New York," *Art in America* 61 (July/August 1973): 59-65; Randall Blackshaw, "The New New York," *Century Magazine* 64 (August 1902): 493-513; and William H. Gerdts, *Impressionist New York* (New York, London, Paris: Abbeville Press, 1994).

33. Gerdts, *Impressionist New York*, p. 8.

34. In *Impressionist New York* (p. 34) Gerdts argues, "The Eight should be seen as an *extension* of the figurative Impressionists — not so radical as the modernists but ready to reinvestigate the tougher, more ugly, sometimes more pessimistic themes of the figurative French Impressionism that had been so emphatically rejected in New York in 1886."

35. "The Impressionists," *Art Age* 3 (April 1886): 165-166, quoted in Gerdts, *Impressionist New York*, p. 34.

36. On this topic, John Sloan recalled that Henri had recently returned from an extended stay in Europe. "He was full of enthusiasms for the work of Manet, and started to talk about the need for painting the everyday world in America just as had been done in France." Sloan is quoted in *American Art Nouveau: The Poster Period of John Sloan* (Lock Haven, PA: Hammermill Paper Co. Lock Haven Division), n.p.

37. Rebecca Zurier, Robert W. Snyder, Virginia M. Mecklenburg, *Metropolitan Lives: The Ashcan Artists and Their New York (Washington, D.C.: National Museum of American Art, 1955)*, p. 14.

38. Barth, *City People*, p. 3.

39. Shinn may have become familiar with pastels while at the Pennsylvania Academy. Thomas P. Anshutz and Hugh Breckenridge, both well known for their use of pastel, were teaching at the Academy during the years of Shinn's enrollment.

40. For the revival of pastels, see Doreen Bolger, Mary Wayne Fritzsche, Jacqueline Hazzi, Gail Stavitsky, Mary L. Sullivan, Marc Vincent, Elizabeth Wylie, "American Pastels, 1880-1930: *Revival & Revitaization,*" in Doreen Bolger, Mary Wayne Fritzsche, Jacqueline Hazzi, Marjorie Shelley, Gail Stavitsky, Mary L. Sullivan, Marc Vincent, Elizabeth Wylie, *American Pastels in the Metropolitan Museum of Art* (New York: The Metropolitan Museum of Art, 1989), pp. 1-32; and Dianne H. Pilgrim, "The Revival of Pastels in Nineteenth-Century America: The Society of Painters in Pastel," *American Art Journal* 10 (November 1978): 43-62.

41. For Shinn's treatment of pastels, see Theodore Stebbins, Jr., *American Master Drawings and Watercolors* (New York, Harper & Row, 1976), p. 278; and Patricia Hills, *Turn-of-the-Century America* (New York: Whitney Museum of Art, 1977), p. 147.

42. From February 4 – 16, 1901 *Fire Scene* was exhibited at the J. Eastman Chase's Gallery in Boston with the title *Downtown Fire*. It was also illustrated in the February 1901 issue of *Century Magazine* with the caption, "Street Scene at a Fire." The pastel is closely related to the illustration of a fire engine that Shinn completed for an article in *Ainslee's Magazine*. Although the backdrops for the fires are vastly diverent, the details of the fire engines and their placement in the compositions are almost identical, demonstrating Shinn's willingness to reuse images in diverent contexts. "Four Midwinter Scenes in New York: From Pastels by Everett Shinn," *Century Magazine* 61 (February 1901): 525; "Modern Fire Fighting," *Ainslee's Magazine* 3 (June 1899): 521.

43. In *American Master Drawings and Watercolors,* (p. 278) Stebbins notes Shinn's possibly ironic use of pastel to render Ashcan subjects. Shinn was not the only Ashcan artist to work in pastel. William Glackens also produced striking works in this medium. See, for example, *Shop Girls* (before 1901; The Metropolitan Museum of Art.

44. SAM.

45. See John Edgar Bullard, "John Sloan and the Philadelphia Realists as Illustrators, 1890–1940," (M.A. Thesis, University of California, Los Angeles, 1968), p. 66. According to Bullard the project caused Shinn to give up his job at *Ainslee's Magazine*.

46. SAM.

47. The quote is taken from an excerpt of a letter written by Everett Shinn. The excerpt, which provides neither the date of the letter nor the identity of its recipient, is in the Shinn file, James Graham & Sons, New York.

48. For a discussion of the books and articles available to Shinn and the other Ashcan artists, see the chapter "The Other Half," in Marianne Doezema, *George Bellows and Urban America* (New Haven and London: Yale University Press, 1992), pp. 123-199; and William R. Taylor, *In Pursuit of Gotham: Culture and Commerce in New York* (New York, Oxford: Oxford University Press, 1992), pp. 78-81.

49. Jacob Riis, *How the Other Half Lives* (New York: Charles Scribner's Sons, 1890; repr., New York: Dover Publications, 1971), p. 83.

50. Matthew Hale Smith, *Sunshine and Shadow in New York* (Hartford, Conn.: J. B. Burr, 1869). Helen Campbell, *Darkness and Daylight in New York* (Hartford, Conn.: The Hartford Publishing Co., 1897).

51. As cited in Ellen Moers, *Two Dreisers* (New York: The Viking Press, 1969), p. 16; full citation for James is not given.

52. Van Wyck Brooks, *Howells, His Life and World* (New York: E. P. Dutton & Co., Inc., 1959), p. 194.

53. SAM.

54. Two exhibitions have assembled several of the "New York by Night" pictures. Virginia E. Lewis, *Everett Shinn, 1876-1953, An Exhibition of His Work*, (Pittsburgh: University of Pittsburgh, 1959). The exhibition included a portfolio of 35 pastels of night scenes planned for "New York by Night." The works were housed in a wooden box made by Shinn and lent by his friend Charles T. Henry. Lewis lists five works by title: *Madison Square Cab Stand*, 1899; *Newspaper Row*, 1899-ca. 1908; *The Fleischman Breadline*, 1900; *All-Night Café*, 1899-ca. 1908; and *Broadway Theater, Julia Marlowe in Barbara Frietchie*, 1899-c.1908. From February 1 to 28, 1958, James Graham & Sons, held an exhibition titled *Everett Shinn*, which showed six pictures from "New York by Night": *News Paper Row*, 1900; *Fleischman Bread-Line*, 1900; *Delmonico's, Fifth Avenue*, 1904; *Lunch Wagon Madison Square*, 1900; *6th Avenue El, After Midnight*, 1899; *Ambulance Call, Winter Night*, 1908.

55. Letter written by Shinn, Shinn file, James Graham and Sons, see footnote 48.

56. A copy of the Library of Congress document is in the Shinn papers at the Delaware Art Museum. Shinn sent a dummy of "New York by Night" to *Harper's* on February 1900, to Brown-Merrell & Co, in Indianapolis in October 1902, and to Grignard Lithographic Co., N.Y. in November 1902; all were returned. Record Book 1, pp. 7, 38. Although "New York by Night" was not published, Shinn never gave upon the idea. In 1950, he revived the concept and was at work on a book chronicling the city that was to include a work titled *The Washington Irving House* (1950; Private Collection). Regarding the picture, he noted "this drawing to be used in Everett Shinn's book, *New York from 1900 to 1950* (book in publication)." Shinn file, James Graham & Sons.

57. Taylor, *In Pursuit of Gotham,* pp. 69-74.

58. Ibid., p. 71.

59. For Madison Square, see *A Historical Sketch of Madison Square* (New York: Meridan Monographs, no. 1, 1894).

60. Bayard Still, *Mirror for Gotham* (New York: New York University Press, 1956), p. 22.

61. *A Historical Sketch of Madison Square*, p. 5.

62. *Baedeker's United States*, edited by Karl Baedeker (Leipsic: Karl Baedeker, 1899), p. 9.

63. Shinn Record Book 1, p. 1.

64. Shinn Record Book 1, pp. 15, 21.

65. "Pastels by Everett Shinn," *Boston Daily Advertiser*, February 7, 1901, Scrapbook, 1898-1906, AAA, roll D179, frame 30.

66. This work is likely the one listed in Shinn's Record Book 1, p. 15 as *Madison Square Cabs.*

67. Wanda Corn has noted that elements such as snow and haze were common devices employed by 19th century artists to soften the perceived harshness of the New York City. See Corn "The New New York," 60.

68. Jesse Lynch Williams, "The Walk Up-Town in New York," *Scribner's Magazine* 27 (January 1900): 53.

69. "Art Notes," *New York Evening Sun*, February 24, 1900, p. 4.

70. According to Shinn's record book, this pastel was originally titled *Fifth Avenue*. The work was once owned by Jeanette Gilder of *The Critic* to whom it may have been given by the artist. Gilder lent it to Shinn's exhibition at Boussod, Valadon & Co. where Charles Allis purchased it. In November of 1900 Shinn gave Gilder a pastel titled *A Rainy Night* possibly in thanks for parting with *Fifth Avenue.* See Record Book 1, pp. 6, 14.

71. "The Dewey Arch," *The American Architect and Building News* 67 Part 1 (January 13 1900): 11-12; "The Dewey Arch," *Architects' and Builders' Magazine* 1 (October 1899): 1-8; *The Encyclopedia of New York City*, ed., Kenneth T. Jackson (New Haven and London: Yale University Press, 1995), p. 331.

72. "The Dewey Arch," *The American Architect and Building News*, p. 12.

73. See, for example, Raffaëlli's *Dewey's Arch, New York* (1899; Private Collection) and Hassam's, *Dewey's Arch* (1900; Private Collection). Both works are illustrated in Gerdts, *Impressionist New York*, p. 83.

74. Clifton Hood, "Subways, Transit Politics and Metropolitan Spatial Expansion," in David Ward and Oliver Zunz, eds., *The Landscape of Modernity: Essays on New York City, 1900–1940* (New York: Russell Sage Foundation, 1992), p. 192.

75. Baedeker, *Baedeker's United States*, p. 11.

76. Ibid., pp. 11-13.

77. William Dean Howells, *A Hazard of New Fortunes* (New York: Harper & Bros. 1899), pp. 158-59.

78. Luc Sante, *Low Life: Lures and Snares of Old New York* (New York: Farrar, Straus, & Giroux, Inc.), p. 50.

79. *Fifth Avenue Stage, Winter* was reproduced in *The Craftsman* with the title *Fifth Avenue Bus in a Snow Storm*. See A. E. Gallatin, "The Pastellists," *The Craftsman* (January 1912): 142-144.

80. "The Storm King Holds Full Sway," *New York Times* (February 14, 1899), front page.

81. For a discussion of the Stieglitz photograph see Moers, *Two Dreisers*, p. 12.

82. Record Book 1, pp. 5-6.

83. Philadelphia *Inquirer*, April 8, 1900, p. 8.

84. *New York Mail & Express*, February 28, 1900, Scrapbook, 1898-1906, AAA, roll D179, frame 8.

85. See, for example, the interpretation of George Luks's painting *Hester Street* in *American Impressionism and Realism: The Painting of Modern Life, 1885 –1915*. The authors interpret the painting as a toned down representation of the poverty and chaos of the Lower East Side. They note, "It is a measure of the editing and euphemism of Luks's painting that the extraordinary clutter of Lower East Side pushcarts…is reduced to this single cart." H. Barbara Weinberg, Doreen Bolger, and David Park Curry, *American Impressionism and Realism: The Painting of Modern Life, 1885 –1915* (New York: Metropolitan Museum of Art and Harry N. Abrams, 1994), p. 192.

86. Zurier and Snyder, *Metropolitan Lives*, pp. 20-27.

87. See Maren Stange, *Symbols of Ideal Life: Social Documentary Photography in America, 1890-1950* (Cambridge, England: Cambridge University Press, 1989), chap. 1, as cited in Zurier and Synder, *Metropolitan Lives*, p. 21.

88. Zurier and Snyder, *Metropolitan Lives*, p. 26.

89. Louis Baury, "The Message of Bohemia," *The Bookman* 34 (November 1911): 256-266.

90. Luc Sante, *Low Life*, pp. 15-16.

91. SAM; The double period configuration, "…", is quoted as written in Shinn's text.

92. Daniel Bluestone, "The Pushcart Evil" in Ward and Zunz, *The Landscape of Modernity*, p. 298.

93. This may be the pastel titled *Park Row* exhibited by Shinn in 1900 at Boussod, Valadon & Co. *Park Row* was noticed by a reviewer who commented, "Mr. Shinn has a well-educated eye for color values, and his *House Tops (rainy day)* (2), *Unloading at the Docks* (16), *Cooper Union Fountain* (22), and *Park Row* (35) show glimpses of brick and building stones seen through a New York winter haze...." *Studio* (New York City) April 1900, Scrapbook, 1898–1906, AAA, roll D179, frame 9. Though *Park Row* was sold during the Boussod, Valadon & Co. exhibition, it traveled with show to the Pennsylvania Academy.

94. The author is indebted to Mr. Christopher Gray for kindly sharing his insight on the location represented in this pastel.

95. The pastel, with its densely packed crowd and attention to pushcart commerce, invites comparison with Luks's painting *Hester Street*. However, unlike *Hester Street* in which couples are engaged in friendly conversation and children are entertained by a peddler demonstrating a toy, *Park Row, Fruit Vendors* overs a more complex view of the urban scene.

96. David Nasaw, *Children of the City: At Work and At Play* (New York: Anchor Press, 1985), pp. 14-15.

97. For a through discussion of this topic, see Bruce Weber, *Ashcan Kids: Children in the Art of Henri, Luks, Glackens, Bellows & Sloan* (New York: Berry-Hill Galleries, 1999).

98. Doezema, *George Bellows*, pp. 154, 159.

99. In addition to the ragpicker pictures mentioned in this essay, other examples by Shinn include *Early Morning Paris* (1901; The Art Institute of Chicago) and *The Ragpicker* (1909; Collection of Mr. and Mrs. Arthur G. Altschul).

100. Sante, *Low Life*, p. 65.

101. Charles Loring Brace, *The Dangerous Classes of New York* (1872), 152-153, quoted in Sante, *Low Life*, p. 66.

102. *Rag Picker* is listed in Shinn's Record Book 1, p. 6. *Ragpicker* is illustrated in Regina Armstrong, "The New Leaders in American Illustration, The Typists: McCarter, Yohn, Glackens, Shinn and Luks," *The Bookman* 11 (May 1900): 249.

103. "Pastels by Everett Shinn," *Boston Daily Advertiser*, February 7, 1901, Scrapbook, 1898-1906, AAA, roll D179, frame 30.

104. "Exhibition of Mr. Shinn's Pastels at Chase's Gallery," *Boston Evening Transcript,* February 6, 1901, 17.

105. "Everett Shinn Pictures," was held at the Morton Galleries, New York, from February 25 – March 9, 1935. *Opening Shop…Paris* is listed as no. 3 under the heading "watercolor."

106. For Elsie de Wolfe, see Jane S. Smith, *Elsie de Wolfe: A Life in the High Style* (New York: Athenaeum, 1982); Elsie de Wolfe, *After All* (New York: Harper, 1935; repr., New York: Arno Press, 1975); and David Park Curry, "Never Complain, Never Explain: Elsie de Wolfe and the Art of Social Change," in *Cultural Leadership in America Art Matronage and Patronage, Fenway Court* 27 (Boston: Trustees of the Isabella Stewart Gardner Museum, 1994): 52-78.

107 Smith, *Elsie de Wolfe*, p. 54.

108. "The Academy Exhibition, Sixty-Eighth Annual Display the Best in Recent Years," Philadelphia *Press*, January 15, 1899, p. 6.

109. *Monitor Register*, Woodstown, January 27-28, 1899, Scrapbook 1898–1906, AAA, roll D179, frame 3.

110. SAM. This quote is copied verbatim including the series of two dots.

111. Shinn Record Book I, pp. 1-3.

112. The exchange was related by Everett Shinn to Bennard Perlman in a conversation on September 12, 1952. As quoted in Perlman, *Painters of Ashcan School: The Immortal Eight*, p. 85.

113. For exhibition dates see, "Art Notes," *New York Mail & Express*, February 24, 1900, p. 8.

114. "The Heart of the Town," unidentified news clipping, Scrapbook 1898-1906, AAA, roll D179, frame 10.

115. SAM.

116. A letter from White to Shinn dated September 17, 1903 reveals that the architect would try to sell Shinn's pastels to people he knew. In return for this kind gesture Shinn offered to give White a picture. White responded, "I am sorry to send back the three pastels, but I hoped to get Col. Payne to take them. I never, however could induce him to give me a definitive answer; but I may be able to do so when he returns. I should buy one myself, if I could afford it, but as for giving me one, you must not think of doing so." Stanford White, New York, to Everett Shinn, New York, 17 September 1903, Stanford White Collection, Avery Library, Columbia University, New York. In a letter to Royal Cortissoz, Shinn wrote of his admiration for and indebtedness to White, "to this day he [White] is rather of a hero to me as he brought about my first exhibition and was my sponsor. As busy a man as he was, he always had time for me, an unknown artist." Everett Shinn, New York, to Royal Cortissoz, New York, 8 Jan. (no year given), Cortissoz Correspondance, Yale Collection of American Literature, Beinecke Rare Book and Manuscript Library, Yale University, New Haven.

117. Armstrong, "The New Leaders in American Illustration," 248-249.

118. *New York Evening Post*, February 24, 1900, p. 7.

119. "The World of Art, The Shinn Pastels Come to the Academy," Philadelphia *Inquirer*, March 25, 1900, p. 8.

120. "The Heart of the Town," unidentified news clipping, Scrapbook 1898-1906, AAA, roll D179, frame 10.

121. Ibid.

122. Chicago *Record-Herald*, June 9, 1901, Scrapbook 1898-1906, AAA, roll D179, frame 37.

123. "The Week in Art," *New York Times,* March 3, 1900, p. 139.

124. "Art News," *New York Evening Post*, February 24, 1900, p. 7.

125. "The Heart of the Town," unidentified news clipping, Scrapbook 1898–1906, AAA, roll D179, frame 10.

126. SAM.

127. For Shinn's impending trip to Europe, see "Art & Artists," the Philadelphia *Press*, March 29, 1900, p. 4; "The World of Art, The Shinn Pastels to Come to the Academy," the Philadelphia *Inquirer*, March 25, 1900, p. 8; and "Art Notes," the Philadelphia *Inquirer*, May 6, 1900, sec. 3, p. 2.

128. There has been some confusion about when Shinn was in Paris. In 1952 a reviewer mistakenly wrote of Shinn's European trip: "He liked it but he never went back; he paints Paris and London today as he saw them in 1903." James Fitzsimmons, "Everett Shinn: Lone Survivor of 'The Ashcan School,'" *The Art Digest* 27 (November 15, 1952): 10. Shinn, however, was definitely in Paris in 1900 as he wrote to his friend Charles T. Henry, "I was in Paris during the Exposition and the date of the Ex — was 1900 — as I made that drawing during my stay there the date would be 1900. Or, else the date of the exposition would have to be changed and only the French Government could do that." Everett Shinn to Charles T. Henry, undated letter, Shinn Archives, Box 1, letters, Yale Collection of American Literature, Beinecke Rare Book and Manuscript Library, Yale University, New Haven.

129. The English subjects exhibited at Boussod, Valadon & Co. from January 15 to February 23, 1901 were: *Green Park London, London Street Chelsea, Afternoon Hyde Park, Trafalgar Square, Near the Strand London,* and *Old London House.* Record Book 1, pp. 16-19.

130. *Impressionism: Paintings Collected by European Museums,* (Atlanta: High Museum of Art, 1998), p. 132.

131. This date is based on the fact that Shinn would have needed at least two weeks to get settled in Paris and paint before his small exhibition at the Paris gallery Goupil's at the beginning of July 1900.

132. Shinn later depicted the street where he once lived in the pastel *Rue Notre Dame Des Champs* (1903; Worcester Art Museum).

133. For artists' studios on Rue Notre Dame des Champs, see John Milner, *The Studios of Paris* (New Haven and London: Yale University Press, 1988), pp. 211-218.

134. SAM. This statement is somewhat problematic as Degas was then living at 37 Rue Victor Massé. It is possible that Shinn had at one time lived on Rue Victor Masse, or perhaps he simply mis-remembered Degas as his neighbor.

135. SAM.

136. Unidentified news clipping, Scrapbook 1898-1906, AAA, roll D179, frame 58.

137. Perlman, *The Immortal Eight*, p. 82.

138. John Milner, *The Studios of Paris*, pp. 211-216.

139. In 1901, Shinn exhibited a pastel titled *Rue de Paris Exposition* at Boussod, Valadon & Co. Record Book 1, p. 16.

140. For an excellent discussion of American Art at the 1900 Paris Exposition, see Diane P. Fisher, ed., *Paris 1900: "The American School" at the Universal Exposition* (New Brunswick, New Jersey, and London: Rutgers University Press, 1999).

141. Robert Henri, *The Art Spirit* (New York: J. B. Lippincott, 1923; repr., Colorado: Westview Press, 1984), p. 123.

142. Record book 1, p. 13. None of these works has been currently located.

143. Smith, *Elsie de Wolfe, A Life in the High Style*, pp. 74-75.

144. This group (including the Shinns) was featured in a photo taken at the De Wolfe/Marbury residence at Versailles. The photo, which is dated (verso) in pencil 1900, is now in the Shinn papers at the Helen Farr Sloan Library, Delaware Art Museum. In 1903, the photo was used in an article in *The Critic* on the Paris salon of Marbury and De Wolfe. The date of the publication has led to misguided speculation that the Shinns may have returned to France in 1903. However, in 1902 de Wolfe and Marbury moved from their small French villa to an English "cottage," which was larger and more suitable for entertaining. By contrast, the residence featured in *The Critic* is described as a French villa where dinner parties are small "owing to the size of the dining room." This evidence suggests that, though published in 1903, the article is based on an earlier visit. Moreover, according to Mary Ellen Kelly, an independent scholar who is researching Belasco (included in the photo), the playwright was not in France in 1903, but was there in 1900 having arrived in Paris within a few days of the closing of his play *Zaza* on July 28, 1900. Belasco returned to the U.S. in August thereby dating the photo to sometime between the end of July and the end of August 1900. In late 1900, Shinn gave De Wolfe a portrait, presumably in thanks for her hospitality in France. *The Critic* 43 (October 1903): 291-296. Smith, *Elsie de Wolfe*, p. 85. Telephone conversation between Mary Ellen Kelly and the author, September 17, 2000. For Belasco's trip to Europe in 1900 see also Craig Timberlake, *The Life and Work of David Belasco, the Bishop of Broadway* (New York: Library Publishers, 1954), pp. 199-203. For De Wolfe's portrait, see Record Book 1, p. 13.

145. "Art Notes," *The Evening Post*, New York, July 16, 1901, p. 4.

146. *Brooklyn Daily Eagle*, January 19, 1901, Scrapbook 1898-1906, AAA, roll D179, frame 28.

147. *The New York Evening Sun*, November 16, 1901, Scrapbook 1898-1906, AAA, roll D179, frame 39.

148. Riter Fitzgerald, "Item," Philadelphia, November 19, 1901, Scrapbook 1898-1906, AAA, roll D179, frame 39.

149. Unidentified clipping, Scrapbook 1898-1906, AAA, roll D179, frame 39.

150. "Art Notes," *New York Evening Post*, October 19, 1901, p. 5.

151. *New York Commercial Advertiser*, November 19, 1901, Scrapbook 1898-1906, AAA, roll D179, frame 39.

152. *Brooklyn Daily Eagle*, July 1901, p. 5.

153. Aline B. Louchheim, "The Last of the Eight Looks Back," *New York Times*, p. 9.

154. Shinn Record Book 1, p. 32. This is possibly *The Ballet Dancer* (1901; Georgia Museum of Art).

155. For Degas's women bathing, see Richard Kendall, *Degas Beyond Impressionism* (London: National Gallery Publications, 1996), pp. 230-231.

156. A. E. Gallatin "Studio Talk," *International Studio* 30 (November 1906): 84, 86.

157. See, for example, *Young Girl Playing with a Dog on Her Bed*, (c. 1775; Alte Pinakothek, Bayerische Staatsgemäldesammlungen, Munich). Reproduced in Jean-Pierre Cuzin, *Jean-Honoré Fragonard, Life and Work* (New York: Harry N. Abrams, Inc., 1988), p. 183.

158. Record Book 1, p. 42.

159. Record Book 1, p. 44.

160. Henri Pène du Bois, "A Fragonard of the Present Time," *New York American*, February 22, 1905, p. 14.

161. "The Transformed Piano," *The Sun*, October 15, 1905, p. 5.

162. Scrapbook 1898-1906, AAA, roll D179, frame 37.

163. The Expert, "Passing Up A Few Facts, Everett Shinn's Original Pastels," *Town Topics*, undated clipping [January – February 1901] Scrapbook 1898-1952, AAA, roll D179, frame 29.

164. For a detailed study of Central Park, see Roy Rosenzweig and Elizabeth Blackmar, *The Park and the People: A History of Central Park* (Ithaca, N. Y., and London: Cornell University Press, 1992).

165. For the most current research on Chase's pictures of Central Park, see Barbara Dayer Gallati, *William Merritt Chase: Modern America Landscapes, 1886-1890* (New York: Brooklyn Museum of Art, 1999).

166. Rosenzweig and Blackmar, *The Park and the People*, 232.

167. "Shinn's Work at Boussod & Valadon's," *New York Sun*, January 15, 1901, Scrapbook 1898-1906, AAA, roll D179, frame 32.

168. The Cheekwood Museum of Art dates this work c. 1920s. However, due to the restrained palette, handling of the conté crayon and subject matter, I believe the pastel probably dates c. 1900. A work titled *Bridle Path Central Park*, which most likely the Cheekwood Museum's picture, was exhibited at Boussod, Valadon & Co. in November 1901, a factor that supports an earlier dating. Record Book 1, p. 30.

169. Rosenzweig and Blackmar, *The Park and the People*, p. 244.

170. Ibid.

171. Henry James, *The American Scene* (Chapman & Hall, 1907; repr., New York: St Martin's Press, Inc., 1987), p. 127.

172. Though the Gibbes Art Museum titles this work *Untitled (Park Scene)* the information museum personnel provided the author refers to it as a "Central Park scene." As Shinn produced several Central Park pictures it is difficult to determine the original title of this pastel but it is possibly *Central Park, N.Y* exhibited at Boussod, Valadon & Co. January 15 to February 23, 1901 or *A By-Path Central Park* exhibited at he same gallery from November 6 to 31, 1901. Record Book 1, pp. 18, 29.

173. "A Ramble in Central Park," *Harper's Magazine* 59 (October 1879): 697.

174. Shinn returned to the subject of Central Park in at least four later pictures. In 1903, he exhibited *Central Park, Winter Afternoon* (Location Unknown) at M. Knoedler & Co. *Central Park* (1915; Fogg Art Museum) is a small work on paper depicting a snow-covered view of the entrance to the park at 73RD Street and Central Park West. Later, in the 1920s, Shinn painted a joyful picture, *May Day Central Park* (Private Collection). In 1949, he completed the watercolor *Central Park Wall, Fifth Avenue* (Private Collection) perhaps his last picture of the park.

175. For an excellent discussion of artists who painted Washington Square see Bruce Weber's forthcoming exhibition and catalogue *Hommage to the Square: Picturing Washington Square, 1889–1965,* (New York: Berry-Hill Galleries, May 2001).

176. Glackens's letters to his wife Edith attest to the desirability of a studio on the Washington Square. He writes, "It would be possible to spend most of the time up in Hartford but I wished to do some painting this summer and I can't take the studio with me. I think it would be a good plan not to stay away entirely from Washington Square. Somebody might swipe it." As quoted in Ira Glackens, *William Glackens and the Ashcan Group* (New York: Horizon Press, 1957), p. 61.

177. Charlotte Moffitt, "An Artist's House in New York," *House Beautiful* (December 1902): 18-22.

178. For the development of Washington Square, see Jerry E. Patterson, *Fifth Avenue: The Best Address* (New York, Rizzoli International Publications, Inc., 1998), pp. 14 –18; and *The WPA Guide to New York* (New York: Random House, 1939; repr., New York: Random House, 1982), pp. 131-135.

179. "What is the Most Beautiful Spot in New York?" *New York Times*, June 18, 1911, magazine sec., pt 5 p. 10.

180. For the building of the arch, see Patterson, *Fifth Avenue: The Best Address*, p. 36.

181. Mariana Griswold van Rensselaer, "Picturesque New York," *Century Magazine* 45 (December 1892): 172

182. Everett Shinn, "Washington Square," Dorothy Seiberling Collection, AAA, roll 794, frame 664.

183. SAM.

184. "What is the Most Beautiful Spot in New York?" pp. 4, 10.

185. The pastel *Washington Square Park with Two Figures* (c. 1899; Location Unknown) is probably Shinn's earliest portrayal of the subject. In 1953 he completed the pen and ink drawing *Washington Square Park* (Location Unknown). He died in May of that year.

186. "Art and Artists," *The Commercial Advertiser*, March 11, 1903, p. 9.

187. Chicago *Record-Herald*, March 22, 1903, Scrapbook 1898-1906, AAA, roll D179, frame 48.

188. Ibid.

189. Ibid.

190. In 1934, Shinn returned to the theme in a pastel titled *Falling Leaves* (1934; Location Unknown). Like *Green Park, London*, the work features down-and-out figures slumped against each other under a tree.

191. Sylvia Yount "Consuming Drama: Everett Shinn and the Spectacular City," *American Art* 6 (Fall 1992): 88.

192. Everett Shinn's notes on *The Ambulance Call*. Dorothy Seiberling Collection, AAA, roll 794, frame 663.

193. Shinn's illustrations of fires for the Philadelphia newspapers include "The Fire at Jeverson and Mascher Streets," Philadelphia *Inquirer*, July 26, 1895; "Scene of the Destructive Fire," Philadelphia *Inquirer*, September 25, 1895; and "Scene of the Fire at Broad and Willow Streets," Philadelphia *Inquirer*, October 2, 1895.

194. Everett Shinn, Interview by Matthews (no first name given), no date, Radio Station WLIB Flatbush Avenue, Brooklyn N.Y. Manuscript located in the Shinn papers, Helen Farr Sloan Library, Delaware Art Museum.

195. Written on a label on the back of *Fire on Mott Street* in Shinn's hand.

196 Hugh Bonner, "Modern Fire Fighting," *Ainslee's Magazine* 3 (June 1899): 520-530.

197. This pastel is in the collection of the Yale University Art Gallery where it is titled *Fire Scene*. However, when the pastel was exhibited from February 4-16, 1901 at J. Eastman Chase's Gallery in Boston it was titled *Down Town Fire*. See Shinn Record Book I, p. 20.

198. This work has traditionally been dated 1907. However, the image was created in May 1902 as an illustration for reproduction in *McClure's Magazine*. See, Harvey J. O'Higgins, "A Change of Profession," *McClure's Magazine* 20 (November 1902): 92-98.

199. Doezema, *George Bellows and Urban America*, p. 113.

200. "Water Color Club," *Advertiser* Boston, March 8, 1901, Scrapbook 1898-1906, AAA, roll D179, frame 32.

201. "Fourteenth Annual Exhibition of the Watercolor Club," Boston *Transcript*, March 2, 1901, Scrapbook 1898-1906, AAA, roll D179, frame 32.

202. *The Wrestlers* and *Prize Fighters* are listed in Record Book 1, pp. 14, 49.

203. Robert A. M. Stern, Gregory Gilmartin and John Montague Massengale, *New York 1900: Metropolitan Architecture and Urbanism, 1890–1915* (New York: Rizzoli International Publications, 1983).

204. Anonymous writer, *Scribner's*, quoted in Robert A. M. Stern et al. *New York 1900: Metropolitan Architecture and Urbanism 1890–1915* (New York: Rizzoli International Publications, Inc., 1983), p. 20.

205. Lewis A. Erenberg, *Steppin' Out, New York Nightlife and the Transformation of American Culture, 1890–1930* (Chicago: Univ. of Chicago Press, 1981), pp. 9-11.

206. Mary Black, *Old New York in Early Photographs* (New York: Dover Publications, Inc., 1973), p. 164.

207. Stern et al., *New York 1900*, p. 224.

298. Glackens, *William Glackens*, p. 57.

299. Everett Shinn, as quoted in Bennard B. Perlman, *Robert Henri: His Life and Art* New York: Dover Publications, 1991), p. 51.

210. Shinn had previously used the tracks of the El as a framing device in *Under the Elevated*, (c. 1899; Whitney Museum of American Art). However, the design was not unique to him. For example, it occurs in the painting *Blue Morning* by George Bellows (1919; National Gallery of Art, Washington, D.C.).

211. "The New Fifth Avenue," *The Architectural Record* 22 (July 1907): 1.

212. Mariana Griswold van Rensselaer, "People in New York," *Century Magazine* 49 (February 1895): 545.

213. E. S. Martin, "New York's Easter Parade," *Harper's Weekly* 49 (April 22, 1905): 566-567.

214. For Shinn's illustrations of the Easter Parade, see "Easter Sunday on Fifth Avenue," *Harper's Weekly* XLIV (December 22, 1900): 1240-1241; "In Front of Saint Patrick's Cathedral on Easter Sunday," *Harper's Weekly* 58 (April 11, 1914): 16-17; and "How Easter Comes in the City," *Scribner's Magazine* 31 (April 1902): 450-451, 2 illus.

215. Alan Trachtenberg, *The Incorporation of America* (New York: Hill and Wang, 1982), p. 130.

216. Lillie Hamilton French "Shopping in New York," *Century Magazine* 61, (March 1901): 649.

217. Other representations of shopping by Shinn include: *Christmas Eve in the Shopping District, Harper's Weekly* 22 (December 1900): 1240-1241; *She was Hovering before the Fatal Window.* Illustration for Owen Johnson, *The Salamander,* Indianapolis, 1914 reproduced in *McClure's,* 1913-1914; *Shop Window, Harper's Weekly* 58 (February 14, 1914): 16-17; and *Slushy Night* (1945; Location Unknown).

218. William Leach, "The Strategists of Display and the Production of Desire," in Simon J. Bonner, ed., *Consuming Visions: Accumulation and Display of Goods in America, 1880-1920* (New York & London: W.W. Norton & Company, 1989), p. 103.

219. Wolfgang Schivelbusch, *Disenchanted Night: The Industrialization of Light in the Nineteenth Century,* Angela Davis, trans. (Berkeley University of California Press, 1988), pp. 142, 148, quoted in David Nasaw, "Cities of Light, Landscapes of Pleasure," in Ward and Zunz *The Landscape of Modernity,* p. 275.

220. Leach, "The Strategists of Display and the Production of Desire," p. 110.

221. Lillie Hamilton French "Shopping in New York," *Century Magazine* 61 (March 1901): 651.

222. Theodore Dreiser, *Sister Carrie* (New York: Doubleday, Page and Co., 1900; repr., New York: Penguin Books, 1981), p. 23.

223. The original titles of these pictures may be *Show Window Rainy Night* and *Shop Window,* respectively. *Show Window* was shown in Shinn's exhibition at Durand-Ruel Galleries, March 2-16, 1904. Shinn sent a work titled *Shop Window* to the Rochester Art Club on November 5, 1904.

224. Leach, "The Strategists of Display and the Production of Desire," pp. 111-113.

225. French "Shopping in New York," 651.

226. Leach, "The Strategists of Display and the Production of Desire," p. 113.

227. Valerie Steele, "Clothing and Sexuality," in *Men and Women: Dressing the Part,* eds. Claudia Brush Kidwell and Valerie Steele (Washington: Smithsonian Institution Press, 1989), pp. 50-51.

228. *Retail Ledger,* June 6 1923, p. 6. *Display World* 49, (August 1946): 90, quoted in Leach, "The Strategists of Display and the Production of Desire," p. 118.

229. Kathy Peiss, "Commercial Leisure and the 'Woman Question," in *For Fun and Profit: The Transformation of Leisure into Consumption,* ed. Richard Butsch (Philadelphia: Temple University Press, 1990), p. 112.

230. Dreiser, *Sister Carrie,* p. 323.

231. "Exhibition of Mr. Shinn's Pastels at Chase's Gallery," *Boston Evening Transcript,* February 6, 1901, p. 17.

232. "Pastels by Everett Shinn," *Boston Daily Advertiser*, February 7, 1901, Scrapbook, 1898-1906, AAA, roll D179, frame 30. While the pastel was on view at J. Eastman Chase's Gallery it also appeared as an illustration in: "Four Midwinter Scenes in New York — From Pastels by Everett Shinn," *Century Magazine* 61 (February 1901): 521-525. The work was reproduced with the caption: *Broadway, Late in the Afternoon.*

233. "Pastels by Everett Shinn," *Boston Daily Advertiser*, February 7, 1901, Scrapbook, 1898–1906, AAA, roll D179, frame 30.

234. Helen H. Henderson, "Philadelphia Artists Exhibiting in New York," *Philadelphia North American* March 11, 1903, Scrapbook, 1898–1906, AAA, roll D179, frame 45.

235. For an excellent account of Shinn's theater subjects, see Linda Ferber, "Stagestruck: The Theater Subjects of Everett Shinn," *American Art Around 1900: lectures in memory of Daniel Fraad.* Edited by Doreen Bolger and Nicolai Cikovsky, Jr. (Washington: National Gallery of Art, 1990). Ferber points out Shinn's attention to the interaction between the audience and the performer.

236. Regarding *Julia Marlowe in Barbara Frietchie* Shinn recalled: "It is Clyde Fitch's play of 'Barbara Frietchie.' The star is Julia Marlowe. Many nights I had stood in the wings watching the performance. One night, Miss Marlowe passed me on an entrance cue complaining that she felt ill and feared she could not get through the act. At a very tense moment when she had evaded the advances of a drunken Yankee seargent [sic]she passed at a table near where I stood. Thrilled by her panic and exhaustion I had forgotten her complaint…. Then I realized she was on the point of fainting. I forgot the play and stepped out on to the stage, my arms extended if she should fall…. Miss Marlowe smiled…My deep concern was forgiven." Everett Shinn, "Behind the Scenes," Everett Shinn Material, Dorothy Seiberling Collection, AAA, roll 794, frame 667.

237. "Art News," *New York Evening Post*, February. 24, 1900, p. 7.

238 "Mr. Shinn's Work at Boussod & Valadon's," *New York Evening Sun*, January 15, 1901, p. 4.

239. The apt description "stagestruck" is taken from the title of Ferber's article: "Stagestruck: The Theater Subjects of Everett Shinn."

240. "Everett Shinn's Pastels," *Brooklyn Daily Eagle* (January 16, 1901) Scrapbook, 1898-1906, AAA, roll D179, frame 28.

241. "Notes on Matters of the Fine Arts," *New York Times*, January 26, 1901, p. 9.

242. Helen W. Henderson, "Philadelphia Artists Exhibiting in New York," *Philadelphia North American*, March 11, 1903, Scrapbook, 1898-1906, AAA, roll D179, frame 45.

243. Everett Shinn's Work," *New York Times,* March 12, 1904, p. 9.

244. The exhibition of the Eight has been extensively covered in art history literature and does not require repeating here. Sources include: William Innes Homer, *Robert Henri and His Circle* (Ithaca and London: 1969); Bennard Perlman, *The Immortal Eight* (New York: Dover Publications, 1979); Mahonri SharpYoung, *The Realist Revolt in American Painting. The Eight* (New York Watson-Guptill, 1973); Elizabeth Milroy, *Painters of a New Century, The Eight* (Milwaukee, Wisconsin: Milwaukee Art Museum, 1991); Judith Zilczer, "The Eight on Tour, 1908-1909," *American Art Journal* 16 (Summer 1984): 20-48.

245. On February 20, 1908, John Sloan wrote in his diary, "All the sales in the exhibition (7) were to three buyers, Mrs. Harry Paine Whitney the rich sculptress — at least she has a fine studio for this purpose — bought four…" Excerpt from John Sloan's diary, as quoted in Everett Shinn material, object file, Whitney Museum of American Art, New York.

246. *The Oxford Companion to the Theater*, edited by Phyllis Hartnoll, third edition (London: Oxford University Press, 1967), p. 444.

247. In order to capture difficult angles, Shinn would often position himself as close as possible to the performers. Although there is no record of Shinn discussing his execution of *The Hippodrome, London*, he did record his experiences years later when he portrayed the Ringling Circus. In a letter to Miss Holzhauer at the Newark Museum, in which he referred to his recent trip to the circus' headquarters, Shinn wrote: "I had a wonderful time and made several sketches of circus life at the Ringling Circus headquarters and at Ringling Hotel where the perfected acts were put on three nights a week for the hotel patrons. It's a great privilege to sit directly under and very close to the performers…." Everett Shinn, New York, to Miss Holzhauer, New Jersey, 8 April, 1949, Object File, The Newark Museum, Newark. The author would like to thank Dr. Holly Pyne Conner, Consulting Curator American Art, The Newark Museum for making this letter available.

248. Record Book 1, p 45.

249. Record Book 1, p 42.

250. "Mrs. Blair," SAM.

251. Record Book 1, p. 57.

252. Weinberg et al. *American Impressionism and Realism*, p. 201.

253. Yount, "Consuming Drama, Everett Shinn and the Spectacular City," 87- 109.

254. Barth, *City People*, pp. 3-5.

255. John E. DiMeglio *Vaudeville U.S.A.* (Bowling Green, Ohio: Bowling Green University Popular Press, 1973), p. 11.

256. Synder, *Voice of the City,* xv.

257. Douglas Gilbert *American Vaudeville: Its Life and Times* (Whittsley House, 1940; repr., New York: Dover Publications, Inc., 1940), p. 4.

258. Synder, *Voice of the City*, p. 12.

259. Everett Shinn, "A Bowery Dance Hall," Everett Shinn Material, Dorothy Seiberling Collection, AAA, roll 794, frame 667.

260. For use of the banjo in vaudeville, see Gilbert, *American Vaudeville, Its Life and Times,* pp. 45-46.

261. Anthony Slide, *The Encyclopedia of Vaudeville* (Westport, CT: Greenwood Press, 1994), p. 278.

262. Snyder, *Voice of the City,* p. 29.

263. Ibid., p. 32.

264. For Proctor's see Synder, *The Voice of the City,* p. 85; and Slide, *The Encyclopedia of Vaudeville,* p. 406.

265. DiMeglio, *Vaudeville U.S.A.,* p. 35.

266. This work was illustrated with the caption: *In Mid-Air.* See Norman Kent, "The Versatile Art of Everett Shinn," *American Artist* (October 1945): 13.

267. Personal note written by Everett Shinn dated 1943 and affixed to the back of the pastel.

268. Slide, *The Encyclopedia of Vaudeville,* p. 352.

269. The original title for the painting may be *"The Funny Man," A London Music Hall Study.* It was reproduced with this title in Louis H. Frohman, "Everett Shinn, the Versatile," *International Studio* 78 (October 1923): 89. For the definition of "Lion Comique" see Wendy Baron and Richard Stone, eds., *Sickert Paintings* (London: Royal Academy of Arts, 1992), p. 64.

270. Baron and Stone, *Sickert Paintings,* p. 64.

271. In the mid-1930s Shinn returned to the theme creating a handful of pictures of funnymen on stage. See for example *The Actor* (1935; St. Bonaventure University), *Man with Top Hat and Cane* (1934; Location Unknown), and *Vaudeville* (1935; Amherst College).

272. Mary Cass Canfield, "The Great American Art," *New Republic* 32 (November 22, 1922): 335, quoted in Snyder, p. 105, footnote 1.

273. See for example: "Wanted Young Man of Athletic Appearance; Must be Good Dresser," *Harper's Weekly* (October 11, 1913): 16-17; "The Artist Failed to Turn Up," *Harper's Weekly* (October 18, 1913): 16-17; and "In Front of Saint Patrick's Cathedral on Easter Sunday," *Harper's Weekly* (April 11, 1914): 16-17.

274. "Art and Artists," *Philadelphia Public Ledger,* March 15 1903, p. 10.

275. An exception to the anonymous dancers are the portraits Shinn executed of the actresses Elsie de Wolfe and Julia Marlowe and two pictures of a female performer named Julie Bonbon. *Julie Bonbon,* 1906–1907, red chalk on paper and *Julie Bonbon,* 1907, pastel on paper, are both in the collection of The Metropolitan Museum of Art.

276. Letter of Everett Shinn, New York, to Ralph H. Norton, Chicago, 14 February 1940, Curatorial file, Norton Museum of Art, West Palm Beach.

277. By the early 1900s Degas's work was immensely well known. His works had been widely exhibited in Europe and significant pictures had been exhibited across the United States largely through the promotion of Durand-Ruel Galleries. Works by Degas entered public and private collections throughout Europe and the United States, where patrons such as the Mr. and Mrs. Havermeyer and Mrs. Potter Palmer prized them. Shinn's knowledge of the artist was fortuitously recapped when in 1901 Durand-Ruel Galleries in New York organized an exhibition of Degas's pastels and oils. For Degas and the marketplace, see Richard Kendall, *Degas beyond Impressionism* (London: National Gallery Publications Limited, 1996), p. 45.

278. Robert L. Herbert *Impressionism: Art Leisure, and Parisian Society* (New Haven and London: Yale University Press, 1988), p. 103.

279. A. E. Gallatin, "Studio-Talk," *International Studio* 30 (November 1906): 84-87.

280. Ibid.

281. Ferber, "Stagestruck: The Theater Subjects of Everett Shinn," 59.

282. George Barry Mallon, "The Hunt for Bohemia," *Everybody's Magazine* 12 (February 1905): 195.

283 Mallon, "The Hunt for Bohemia," 195.

284. For American artists in Spain, see M. Elizabeth Boone, *Espana, American Artists and the Spanish Experience* (New York: Hollis Taggart Galleries, 1999). Boone notes that when Henri's pictures of Spanish dancers were exhibited they were linked by critics to Sargent's *El Jaleo.*

285. For Manet's treatment of Spanish performers, see Herbert, *Impressionism, Art, Leisure, & Parisian Society*, pp. 94-96.

286. Ferber, *Stagestruck: The Theater Subjects of Everett Shinn*," 59. Shinn maintained his interest in Spanish themes as is evident in *Carmen* (1938; Private Collection).

287. For Spanish dancing, see J. E. Crawford Flitch, *Modern Dancing and Dancers* (Philadelphia: L. B. Lippincott Co., 1912), pp. 189-199.

288. As Robert Synder notes, "Some acts were recognized for their ability to draw women. Among them was Ethel Levey, who in her 'gorgeous' costume was apparently the big attraction that drew a crowd 'composed principally of women' to a Harlem Opera House matinee in 1907..." Synder, *Voice of the City*, p. 33, footnote 35.

289. *A Spanish Song* was exhibited at Durand-Ruel Galleries in March 1904. Shinn Record Book 1, p. 48.

290. Shinn Record Book 1, p. 57.

291. Shinn Record Book 1, p. 66.

292. Although the illustration is not titled, it
most likely portrays *The Leader of the
Orchestra*. As had been previously mentioned it is often difficult to determine the
original title of Shinn's paintings as titles
changed depending on the exhibition or
the review. Identification of the painting is
further confused by the fact that the work
was illustrated in *The World Magazine's*
review of The Eight exhibition with the
title *The Duet*, a title not included in The
Eight catalogue. "New York's Art War and
The Eight 'Rebels,'" *The World Magazine*,
February 2, 1908, Undated Scrapbook,
AAA, roll 952, frame 316.

293. SAM.

294. Everett Shinn, New York, to Miss
Holzhauer, New Jersey, 8 April 1949,
Object File, The Newark Museum,
Newark.

295. "Everett Shinn, 79, Noted Artist, Dies,"
New York Times, May 3, 1953, p. 89.

296. "Notes on Various Subjects," SAM.

PLATE I. *Woman at the Chicken Coop*, 1899 113

114   PLATE 2. *A Rainy Day in Madison Square*, 1898

PLATE 3. *Hansom Cabs in Snow*, c. 1899   115

116   PLATE 4. *Park Scene*, 1899

PLATE 5. *Madison Square, Dewey Arch*, 1899 117

PLATE 6. *Horsedrawn Bus*, 1899

PLATE 7. *Fifth Avenue*, c. 1899

119

PLATE 8. *Cooper Square*, C. 1900-1908

PLATE 9. *Park Row, Fruit Venders*, c. 1899   121

122   PLATE 10. *Green Park, London, 1908*

PLATE II. *Street Corner in Paris*, 1905   123

PLATE 12. *Girl in Bathtub*, 1903

PLATE 13. *Boudoir Scene*, 1907

126   PLATE 14. *Young Woman in Her Boudoir*, 1912

PLATE 15. *At the Fountain*, C. 1925   127

PLATE 16. *The East River at Night*, 1906   129

130   PLATE 17. *Nocturne, Gramercy Park*, 1901

PLATE 18. *Election Banner, Madison Square*, 1903   131

PLATE 19. *Spring Shower in Luxembourg Park, Paris,* 1902

PLATE 20. *Washington Square after the Rain*, C. 1902–1903

134   PLATE 21. *Stormy Night in Washington Square*, C. 1910

PLATE 22. *The Arch, Washington Square*, 1929

136   PLATE 23. *Fire on Mott Street*, 1902

PLATE 24. *The Fight*, 1899

PLATE 25. *Delmonico's Fifth Avenue,* 1904

PLATE 26. *Mouquins,* 1904

PLATE 27. *Easter Sunday, Saint Patrick's Cathedral*, 1900   141

PLATE 28. *The Shop Window*, C. 1903

PLATE 29. *Broadway, Late in the Afternoon, After the Matinee*, 1899

144   PLATE 30. *Paris Street Scene #1*, 1902

PLATE 31. *Paris Street Scene, Winter*, 1910

146   PLATE 32. *Broadway Theater: Julia Marlowe in Barbara Frietchie*, 1899–1900

PLATE 33. *At the Hippodrome*, c. 1900

PLATE 34. *Brella*, 1902

PLATE 35. *In the Loge*, 1903   149

PLATE 36. *Girl in Red on Stage*, c. 1905

PLATE 37. *Bowery Music Hall*, 1904   151

152   PLATE 38. *Theater Scene*, 1903

PLATE 39. *Trapeze Artists (Proctor's Theater)*, 1940 153

PLATE 40. *London Music Hall*, 1918

PLATE 41. *At the Stage Door*, 1915   155

PLATE 42. *Singer in White at Piano*, 1913

PLATE 43. *The Black Dress*, c. 1945

158   PLATE 44. *Woman on a Stage*, c. 1910

PLATE 45. *Paris Stage*, 1907   159

PLATE 46. *A French Music Hall,* 1906

PLATE 47. *At the Performance*, 1903   161

162   PLATE 48. *Revue*, 1908

PLATE 49. *Spanish Music Hall*, 1902

PLATE 50. *Keith's Union Square*, c. 1906

PLATE 51. *Girl on Stage*, 1906   165

166   PLATE 52. *Theater Scene*, C. 1906

PLATE 53. *Curtain Call*, 1925   167

PLATE 54. *Outdoor Stage, Paris,* undated

PLATE 55. *The Clown (No Laughs),* 1935   169

List of Plates
in Chronological Order

Broadway Theater: Julia Marlowe in
Barbara Frietchie, c. 1899 – 1900
Watercolor and pastel on paper
8 x 12 inches
Collection of Dr. and
Mrs. David A. Skier
PLATE 32

A Rainy Day in Madison Square, 1898
Pastel on paper
17½ x 21½ inches
Collection of the Charles Allis
Art Museum
PLATE 2

Broadway, Late in the Afternoon, After the
Matinee, 1899
Pastel, charcoal, gouache and watercolor
on artist's board
21¾ x 29½ inches
Private Collection
PLATE 29

The Fight, 1899
Watercolor and ink on paper
8½ x 13⅛ inches
Berry-Hill Galleries, New York
PLATE 24

Horsedrawn Bus, 1899
Pastel on paper
21¾ x 29⅝ inches
The Mr. and Mrs. James McGlothlin
Collection
PLATE 6

Madison Square, Dewey Arch, 1899
Pastel on paper
20½ x 28½ inches
Private Collection
PLATE 5

Park Scene, 1899
Pastel on paper
20 x 28½ inches
Collection of Mrs. James H. Fogelson
PLATE 4

Woman at the Chicken Coop, 1899
Pastel on artist's board
17¼ x 22½ inches
Private Collection
PLATE I

Fifth Avenue, c. 1899
Mixed media on illustration board
19½ x 15½ inches
Private Collection
PLATE 7

Hansom Cabs in Snow, c. 1899
Pastel on paper
21½ x 27 inches
Private Collection, New York
PLATE 3

Park Row, Fruit Venders, c. 1899
Mixed media on paper
17 x 23½ inches
Private Collection
PLATE 9

Easter Sunday, Saint Patrick's Cathedral,
1900
Watercolor, gouache,
and pencil on paper
5½ x 8½ inches
Private Collection
PLATE 27

At the Hippodrome, c. 1900
Charcoal on paper
14 x 20 inches
Private Collection
PLATE 33

Cooper Square, c. 1900-1908
Mixed media on illustration board
14½ x 18½ inches
Private Collection
PLATE 8

Nocturne, Gramercy Park, 1901
Pastel on paper
9⅝ x 13½ inches
Collection of Mr. and Mrs. Stephen M.
Sessler
PLATE 17

Brella, 1902
Pastel on paper
10½ x 15 inches
Collection of Dr. and Mrs. David A.
Skier
PLATE 34

Fire on Mott Street, 1902
Pastel, watercolor, and ink on paper
7⅝ x 13 inches
Private Collection, Courtesy of
Richard York Gallery, New York
PLATE 23

Paris Street Scene #1, 1902
Oil on canvas
10 x 12 inches
Mr. and Mrs. Abbot W. Vose, Vose
Galleries of Boston, Inc.
PLATE 30

Spanish Music Hall, 1902
Oil on canvas
13¾ x 17¾ inches
The Metropolitan Museum of Art,
Bequest of Miss Adelaide Milton de
Groot (1876 – 1967), 1967 (67.187.139)
Photograph © 1993
The Metropolitan Museum of Art
PLATE 49

Spring Shower in Luxembourg Park, Paris,
1902
Pastel on paper
14 x 21¾ inches
Hevrdejs Collection
PLATE 19

Washington Square after the Rain,
c. 1902 – 1903
Pastel on paper
14 x 18 inches
John and Margot Ernst
PLATE 20

At the Performance, 1903
Pastel on artist's board
15 x 20 inches
Private Collection
PLATE 47

Election Banner, Madison Square, 1903
Pastel on paper
23 x 15½ inches
Private Collection
PLATE 18

Girl in Bathtub, 1903
Pastel on paper
16 x 14 inches
Private Collection
PLATE 12

In the Loge, 1903
Oil and pastel on canvas
laid down on board
25½ x 17⅛ inches
Private Collection
PLATE 35

Theater Scene, 1903
Watercolor on paper
heightened with white
14 x 18 inches
Private Collection
PLATE 38

The Shop Window, c. 1903
Pastel on paper
12¼ x 14 inches
Private Collection
PLATE 28

Bowery Music Hall, 1904
Mixed media on paper
8 x 12¾ inches
Private Collection
PLATE 37

Delmonico's Fifth Avenue, 1904
Charcoal, blue and white chalk on paper
8½ x 13½ inches
Private Collection
PLATE 25

Mouquins, 1904
Pastel on cardboard
18¾ x 22⅝ inches
Collection of the Newark Museum,
purchase 1949, Arthur Egner
Memorial Fund
PLATE 26

Street Corner in Paris, 1905
Pastel, ink and wash on paper
9½ x 12 inches
Private Collection
PLATE 11

Girl in Red on Stage, c. 1905
Oil on canvas
17½ x 20 inches
Private Collection
PLATE 36

The East River at Night, 1906
Gouache and pastel on paper
13 x 20½ inches
Slong and Midas Properties, Inc.
PLATE 16

A French Music Hall, 1906
Oil on canvas
21¹⁄₁₆ 29⅜ inches
Collection of Daniel and Rita Fraad
PLATE 46

Girl on Stage, 1906
Red chalk and gouache on paper
13 x 17⅜ inches
Private Collection
PLATE 51

Keith's Union Square, c. 1906
Oil on canvas
20⅜ x 24⅜ inches
Brooklyn Museum of Art
Dick S. Ramsay Fund 42.6
PLATE 50

Theater Scene, c. 1906
Oil on canvas
28¾ x 36 inches
Manoogian Collection
PLATE 52

Boudoir Scene, 1907
Pastel on paperboard
16½ x 17½ inches
Slong and Midas Properties, Inc.
PLATE 13

Paris Stage, 1907
Pastel on board
15 x 17½ inches
Private Collection
PLATE 45

Green Park, London, 1908
Pastel on board
14 x 18 inches
Mr. and Mrs. Meyer P. Potamkin
PLATE 10

Revue, 1908
Oil on canvas
18 x 24 inches
Collection of Whitney Museum of
American Art, Gift of Gertrude
Vanderbilt Whitney; Photograph copy-
right © 1996: Whitney Museum of
American Art, New York
PLATE 48

Paris Street Scene, Winter, 1910
Pastel on paper
16 x 20 inches
Collection of Julie Chase
PLATE 31

Stormy Night in Washington Square,
c. 1910
Watercolor and gouache on glazed paper
9½ x 17 inches
Private Collection
PLATE 21

Woman on a Stage, c. 1910
Oil on canvas
12 x 10 inches
Mr. and Mrs. Eugene A. Gargaro, Jr.
PLATE 44

Young Woman in Her Boudoir, 1912
Pastel on paper
10¾ x 14½ inches
The FORBES Magazine Collection,
New York
PLATE 14

Singer in White at Piano, 1913
Pastel and watercolor on paper
14 x 10 inches
Collection of Mr. and Mrs. Henry
Schwob
PLATE 42

At the Stage Door, 1915
Charcoal and gouache on paper
13¾ x 18¾ inches
Private Collection
PLATE 41

London Music Hall, 1918
Oil on canvas
10 x 12 inches
The Metropolitan Museum of Art,
George A. Hearn Fund, 1921 (21.39)
Photograph © 2000,
The Metropolitan Museum of Art
PLATE 40

Curtain Call, 1925
Oil on canvas
9¼ x 11¼ inches
Berry-Hill Galleries, New York
PLATE 53

At the Fountain, c. 1925
Pastel on paper
18 x 22 inches (sight)
Private Collection
PLATE 15

The Arch, Washington Square, 1929
Watercolor and pastel on board
12¼ x 18⅛ inches
Private Collection
PLATE 22

The Clown (No Laughs), 1935
Oil on canvas
36 x 42 inches
James Graham and Sons
PLATE 55

Trapeze Artists (Proctor's Theater), 1940
Pastel on paper
19½ x 15¼ inches
Collection of David and Rhoda Chase
PLATE 39

The Black Dress, c. 1945
Pastel on board
15⅜ x 11½ inches
Private Collection
PLATE 43

Outdoor Stage, Paris, undated
Pastel on paper
11 x 12⅝ inches
Private Collection
PLATE 54

Copyright © Berry-Hill Galleries, Inc., 2000
Library of Congress Control Number:
00-135420

DESIGN
Anthony McCall Associates, New York

PRINTING
Parker Communications Group, New Jersey

PHOTO CREDITS
Helga Photo Studio, New Jersey
P. Richard Eells, PLATE 2

PAGE 2
Photograph of Everett Shinn, 1907 (DETAIL)

PAGE 6
Girl in Red on Stage, c. 1905 (DETAIL)
Oil on canvas
18 x 21 inches
Private Collection
(PLATE 36)

FRONT COVER
In the Loge, 1903 (DETAIL)
Oil and pastel on canvas laid down on board
25½ x 17⅛ inches
Private Collection
(PLATE 35)

BACK COVER
The Fight, 1899 (DETAIL)
Watercolor and ink on paper
8½ x 13⅛ inches
Berry-Hill Galleries
(PLATE 24)